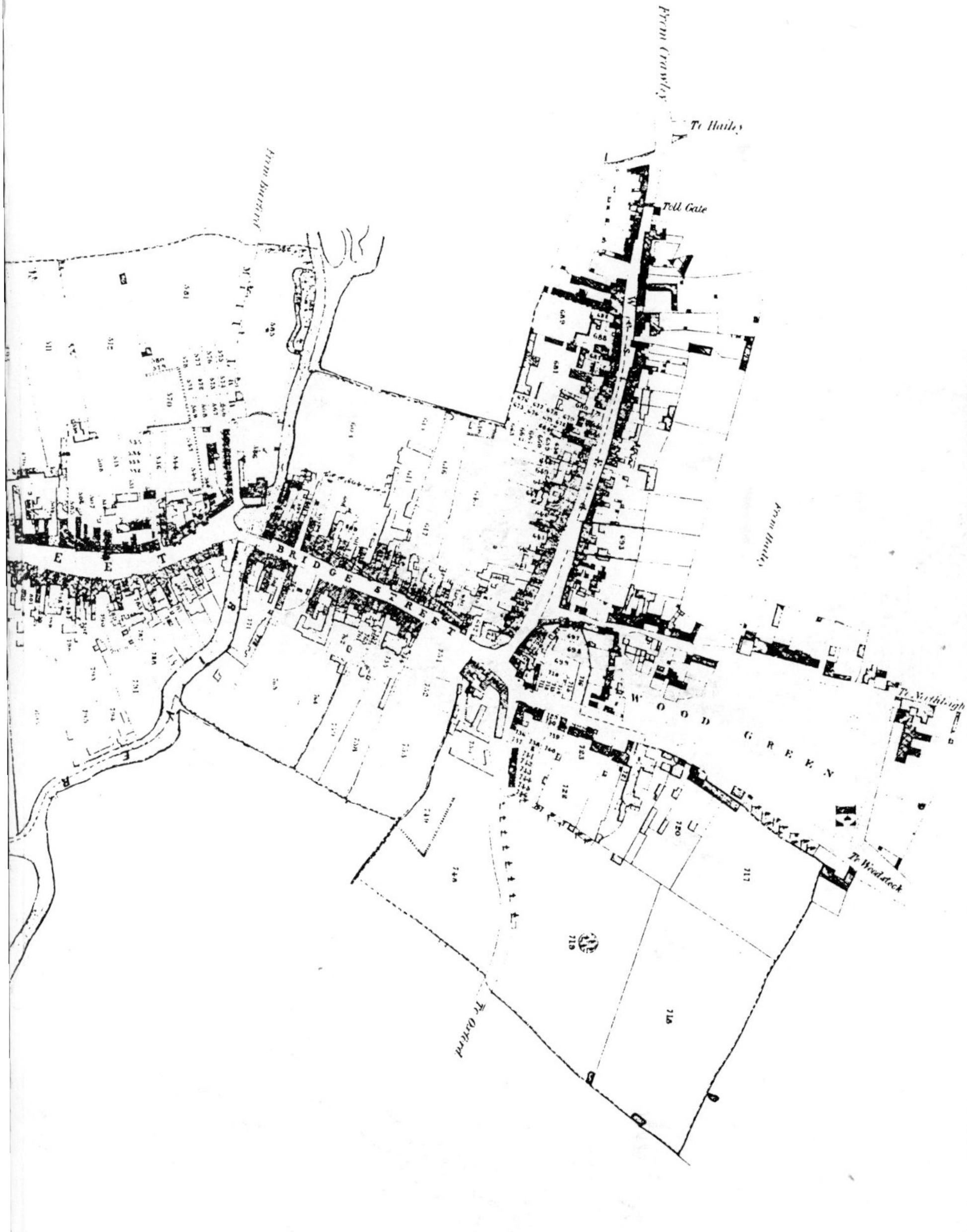

THE BOOK OF WITNEY
Revised edition 1994

FRONT COVER: The High Street, 1828, painted by S. Jones. The originals hang in the Gallery room of the Corn Exchange. Reproduced by permission of Witney Town Council. (AT)

St Mary's Church from The Leys, showing the avenue of young lime trees leading down to the station, c1890. (OCL)

THE BOOK OF WITNEY
(Revised Edition)

by

CHARLES and JOAN GOTT

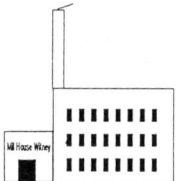

MILL HOUSE PUBLICATIONS, WITNEY.
59 Weavers Close, Witney, Oxfordshire, England
MCMXCIV

Printed by
The WINDRUSH PRESS
Witney, Oxfordshire

PUBLISHED IN 1986 BY BARRACUDA BOOKS
and in this revised edition by
MILL HOUSE PUBLICATIONS, WITNEY
in association with Quotes Limited of Whittlebury.

Copyright © Charles and Joan Gott, 1994

All rights reserved. No part of this publication may be reproduced, stored in a retrieval system, or transmitted, in any form or by any means, electronic, mechanical, photocopying, recording or otherwise, without the prior permission of Mill House Publications, Witney.

ISBN 0 9524405 0 4

DEDICATION

For all the people who are working towards establishing the West Oxfordshire Museum Centre.

CONTENTS

ACKNOWLEDGEMENTS 8

FOREWORD BY R. E. EARLY, MASTER WEAVER OF WITNEY 9

PREFACE BY EILEEN YOUNG, MAYOR OF WITNEY 1984-1986 10

THE OLD FASHIONED TOWN 11

BEFORE THE SAXONS 13

THE WINCHESTER CONNECTION. 17

THE POOR ARE ALWAYS WITH US 29

BOX AND BLUECOAT. 37

WARP AND WEFT 47

GOD'S HOUSE 63

THE DISSENTERS 69

FUN AND GAMES 77

CROSSROADS 85

WITNEY AT WAR 91

OF COURT AND COUNCIL 101

IN BUSINESS 111

EPILOGUE 130

BIBLIOGRAPHY 133

INDEX 135

ACKNOWLEDGEMENTS

This Revised Edition of the Book of Witney is published by kind permission of Clive Birch, Director of Barracuda Press and publisher of the First Edition. Without Clive's initial push we would never have put pen to paper, and for that we thank him.

Many different sources have been used to compile this book. Although no complete history of Witney has been published since 1894, many people have been busy delving into various aspects of life in the town over the past centuries. D. Cross's notes on articles of historical interest in the *Witney Gazette*, as well as his own articles in the same newspaper in the early 1960s, have proved a fruitful source of information. No-one attempting to write a history of Witney would want to be without the valuable and regular contributions to *Record of Witney* made by its Editor, Stanley Jenkins. Many other writers in that journal have provided ideas and information, especially Trevor Cooper.

Very special thanks go to Tom Worley, who has systematically gathered very nearly every known photograph and illustration of Witney, and allowed us to plunder his collection without restraint. Mr and Mrs L. Seely very generously lent us some drawings and other material. We also thank Arthur Titherington for help in the production of some of the photographs. The friendly service of the Evenlode Press has helped enormously in the production of the maps. Kate Steane, who drew the first three maps and the detailed reconstruction of the Bishop's Palace, deserves our special thanks.

The staff of the Oxfordshire Record Office, the Oxfordshire Museum Services, the Oxfordshire Archaeological Unit and the Westgate Local History Library have all been most helpful. We would also like to thank the staff of the Witney Library and the other local public libraries who took so much trouble in helping to organise the first limited edition.

Family records are of great importance in writing a local history. Our sincere thanks go to David Smith, Captain and Mrs Swann, Richard Early, John Dossett-Davies, Richard Adams and Michael Druce for the loan of family and business documents. We have also obtained useful information from Peter Davis, Ray Cripps, Arthur Bissell, R.W. Hawkes and Rev P.J. Taylor. Many other people in Witney have given us ideas, information and encouragement, and we should like to thank them all.

We are grateful to Mr H.E. Green for allowing us to visit Henry Box School, to Alan Crawford for giving us permission to see the archives of Early's of Witney and to Mrs Jean Grace for her invaluable help during that visit. We thank John Kempton for his patience and skill in proof-reading: any mistakes are ours, not his.

Our formal thanks for permission to reproduce copyright material go to the Bodleian Library, the Ashmolean Museum, the British Library, the Oxfordshire County Library Services and the *Oxford Mail*.

FOREWORD TO THE 1986 EDITION

By R. E. Early, Master Weaver of Witney

Like some others among the present fifteen thousand inhabitants of Witney, I can trace our family history in the town back some hundreds of years. We have, therefore, good reason to be grateful to the authors of *The Book of Witney* for the wide-ranging history that follows. Almost as interested will be the newcomers. There must be a large number of these. When I was a boy there were not many more than three thousand men, women and children within our boundaries - and, in general, families seventy-five years ago were larger than they are now!

This book emphasises what the Town owes to the Church. In AD 1044 King Edward the Confessor granted Royal land at Wyttenige to Alfwine, Bishop of Winchester, whose immediate successor Stigand built the Palace, above the foundations of which several families of blanket makers have recently made their homes. I suppose it is because of blankets that Witney is chiefly known throughout the world. I have no reason to disagree with Joan and Charles Gott when they state that by AD 1278 three hundred and seventy sheep were kept on land at Witney, owned by the then Bishop of Winchester, and that by the fourteenth century this number had increased to nearly fifteen hundred. Thus encouraged, clothmaking in Witney by hand and water increased until, in comparatively modern times, the Industrial Revolution took over and 'stocks', 'power looms', 'gigs' and then 'fiberweavers' were introduced.

As the authors do not bring us quite up to date, perhaps I may add that the chief trades and crafts of Witney continue to derive strength from the many other worth-while endeavours by Witney folk described in this book.

PREFACE TO THE 1986 EDITION

By Eileen Young, Mayor of Witney, 1984-1986

Witney has been described as 'that sleepy little market town nestling in the Cotswolds'. Readers of this excellent, comprehensive history of the town compiled by Charles and Joan Gott will soon realise just how inaccurate the adjective 'sleepy' is.

Names from the past will come alive in each chapter as the authors take us from the Bronze Age through to the 20th century and, having embellished their text with many illustrations, give us a full record and insight into the past.

The town of Witney has long been famous for its manufacture of blankets. The section on Industry and Commerce shows how the town can and has produced a lot more besides, proving the Latin inscription on the Town Crest, 'Ingenio Floremus' - by our industry we flourish - to be most apt.

Whilst I was Mayor of Witney I realised how forward-looking Witneans of the past and present have been. Charles and Joan's delightful book proves the town has a firm foundation for its townspeople to build a bright and optimistic future.

PREFACE TO THE 1994 REVISED EDITION

In producing this paperback version of The Book Of Witney, we have made a few amendments to the text, in response to readers' comments and corrections. We have also omitted a small number of illustrations, in order to keep the book to an acceptable size and price.

THE OLD-FASHIONED TOWN

There's an old-fashioned house in an old-fashioned street
In a quaint little old-fashioned town.
There's a street where the cobblestones harass the feet
As it struggles uphill and then down;
And though to and fro through the world I must go
My heart while it beats in my breast
Where'er I may roam, to that old-fashioned home
Will fly back like a bird to its nest.

In that old-fashioned house in that old-fashioned street
Dwell a dear little old-fashioned pair.
I can see their two faces so tender and sweet
And I love every wrinkle that's there.
I love every mouse in that old-fashioned house
In the street that runs uphill and down,
Each stone and each stick, ev'ry cobble and brick
In that quaint little old-fashioned town.

Song written in 1914 by Ada Leonora Harris. (Reproduced by kind permission of Paul E. Harris)

The old-fashioned house in West End where the old-fashioned pair, Charles and Maria Harris lived. They were the uncle and aunt of Ada Leonora Harris.

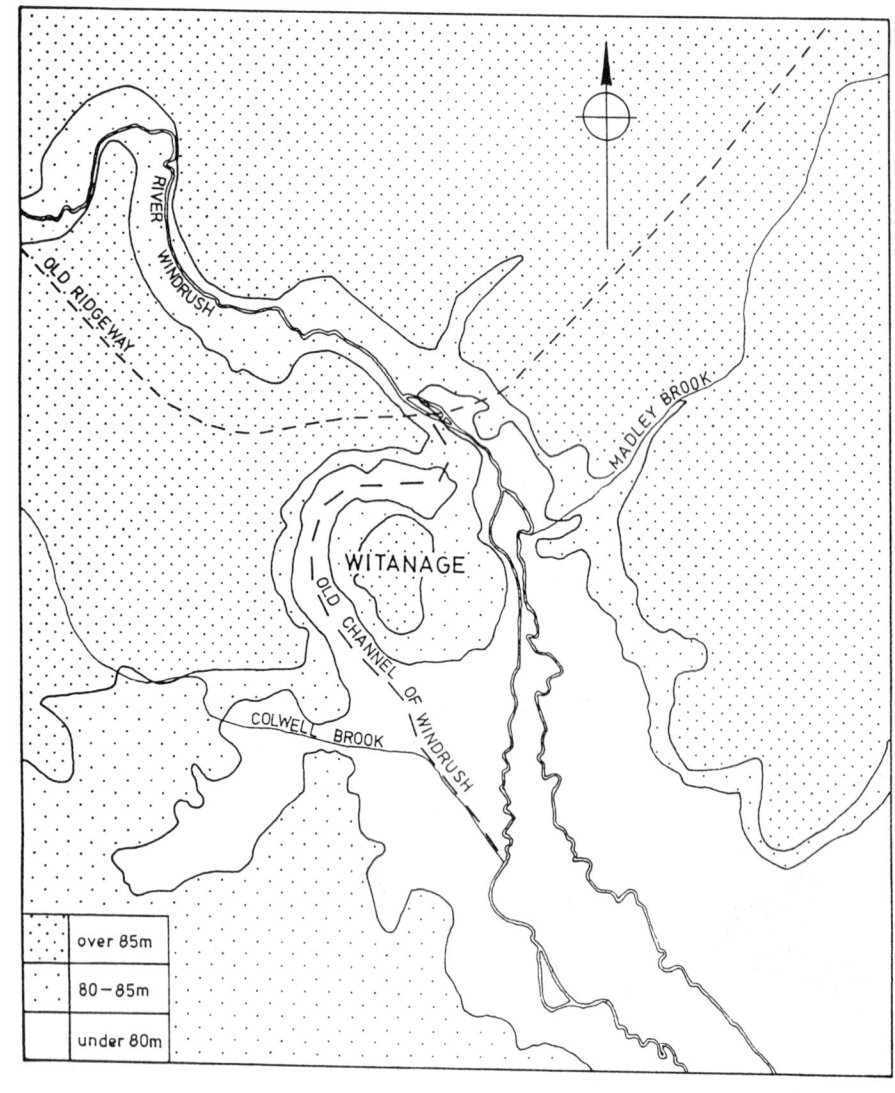

Topography of Witney. (KS)

BEFORE THE SAXONS

Anyone searching for the earliest origins of the town of Witney is forced to stop short at AD 969, for this is the date of the first known written record of the name. It was the year when King Edgar signed a charter granting some land at Wyttanige to a thegn called Oelfhelm. Later, in 1044, the name was spelt Wittannige, and in the Domesday Book (1086) it becomes Witenie.

The original town stands on the westerly side of the river Windrush. Over the centuries it has expanded to meet the settlement on the easterly side, called Cogges, which is now part of the modern town of Witney. Cogges, formerly spelt Coges and Cogas, has an interesting history of its own though, as in the case of Witney, it cannot be traced back further than the 10th century.

Local historian W.J. Monk, who published his *History of Witney* in 1894, suggested that the name could mean island of the Witan, or council of Saxon chiefs. Although this is an attractive idea, the fact that no significant Saxon remains have been found in Witney makes it unlikely. More recent historians lean towards Witta's Island - Witta, it is assumed, being an important Saxon chieftain.

Why island, when the site seems firmly attached to land on most sides? In fact, in Saxon times it really was virtually an island. The town stands on a small rise overlooking the river Windrush. The river runs round two sides of this rise, and the other two sides would have been marshland in those days, making access difficult.

To the north of the site are the rolling Cotswold Hills, which were covered in woods in early times: some of the woodland still remains in the form of the Wychwood Forest. To the south of Witney are the gravel terraces of the Thames valley, well-drained, easily cultivated land that must have been cleared of trees at an early stage, judging from the large number of Iron Age settlements to be found in the area.

Where the Windrush runs through the town, its bed is of rock, making Witney an ideal place for a ford across the river. To the north-east and south-west of the town the river valley widens out, leaving the Windrush running sluggishly and deep over a clay bottom, without any suitable places for fords.

In earlier times the river looked rather different from today's peaceful, disciplined stream. Except where the valley was narrow and stony, it wandered through marshy ground which was flooded in winter, while in hot summers it would have shrunk to a trickle. We do not know when the Windrush was first drained and took its present course, but by Saxon times drainage work was well in hand, and two mills were situated on its banks. A new drainage ditch, which is probably Em's Ditch, had been dug by the year 1044.

There was probably a trackway running along the southern edge of the Cotswold Hills from prehistoric times: part of it is on the old A40 road between Witney and Burford. This track would have crossed the river Windrush near Witney.

The area round present-day Witney was well-settled from the earliest times. Many Neolithic long barrows are to be found in the surrounding country. Near Stanton Harcourt there was a Neolithic henge monument, known as the Devil's Quoits. It has now vanished as a result of gravel workings and a wartime airfield. There are plans to restore it. Bronze and Iron Age sites have been found in the gravel terraces to the south of Witney but, although it is fairly certain that the region was well-populated for at least 2000 years before the coming of the Romans, no evidence

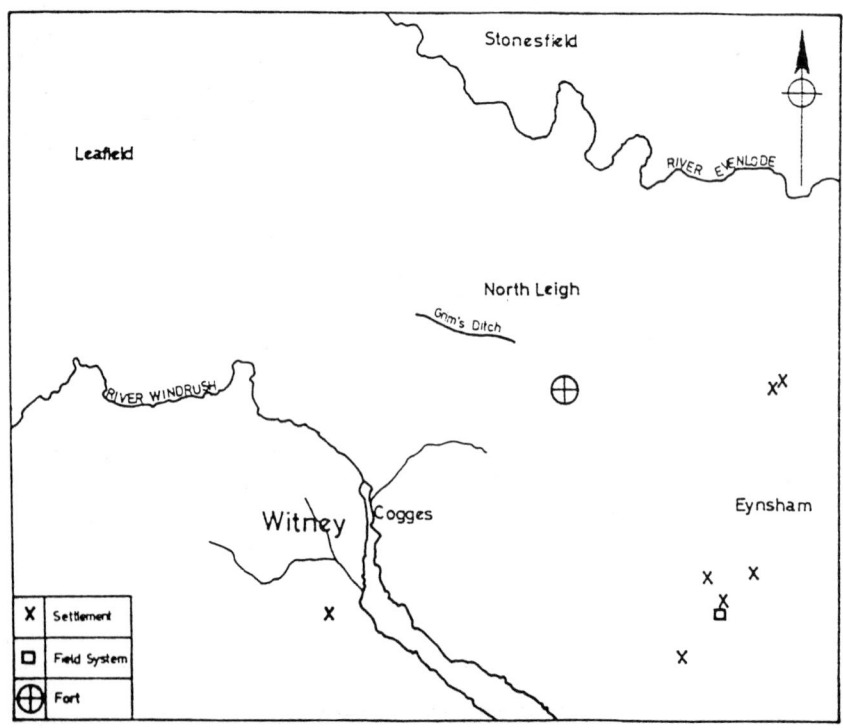

Iron Age sites around Witney. (KS)

has yet been unearthed to prove that there was ever any Bronze or Iron Age occupation of the actual site of today's town. It is true that a bronze dagger was found near Em's Ditch during the building of some new houses, but this find - though interesting - does not prove that people lived there, only that someone dropped his dagger, perhaps while travelling through.

The Romans had a strong presence in the region, setting up numerous villas within a few miles of Witney. The main one was at North Leigh, three miles to the north of the town. The important Roman Akeman Street crosses the Windrush at Asthall, about four miles upstream.

The nearest Roman site is a burial ground discovered during the construction of the Witney by-pass. So, in spite of all the signs of Roman occupation in the area, there is no indication that there was ever any Roman settlement on the site of Witney itself. However, lack of evidence does not necessarily mean that it did not exist: we just do not know.

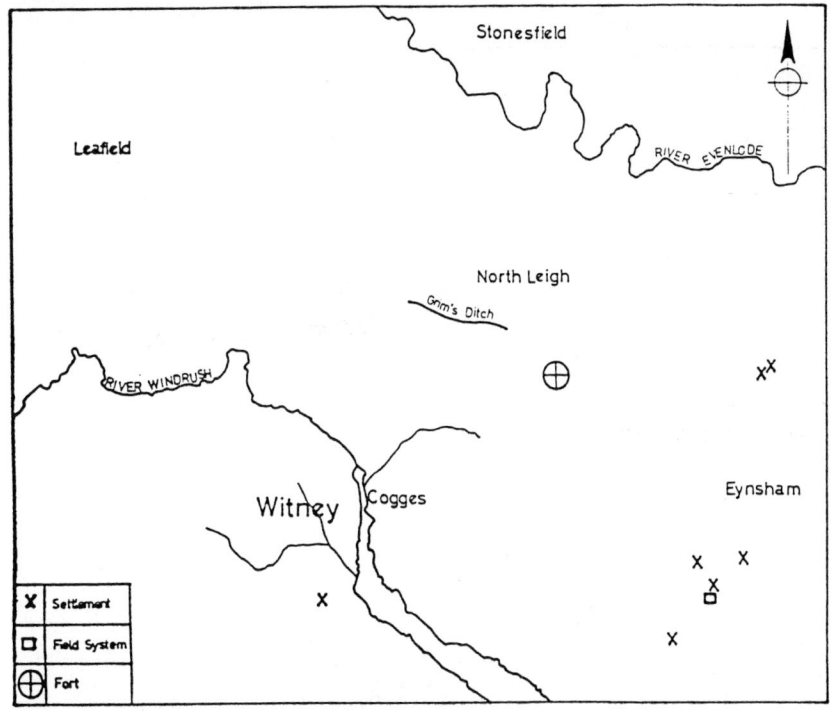

Roman sites around Witney. (KS)

The Bishop's Palace excavation under its protective covering. (JG)

THE WINCHESTER CONNECTION

During the tenth century, a period of considerable unrest, King Edgar divided up his large estate of Bampton, granting the north eastern portion to one of his thegns, Oelfhelm, presumably in order to keep him on his side. In the year 969 the King signed a charter confirming this gift of a large tract of land at Wyttannige. It was made up of 30 hides: enough land to support 30 families. The land coincides with the modern parishes of Hailey, Crawley and Curbridge, as the charter shows, listing all the landmarks to be found round its perimeter.

'These are the land boundaries of the 30 hides at Witney. First from Hawk's mound to the Windrush to the willow row to nut cliff; from the cliff to high lea; from there to long lea road [the road to Langley]; along the road then to chip-lea [a clearing where there are wood-chippings]; then to chip road; along the road where it runs to the north part of the King's promontory; from there to marsh-clearing; along the clearing to Hunter's Road; along the road to where it comes out at the dwelling-place; from there always along the lower side to Ofling acre; from there to the old road; along the road to Cyga's stone; from the stone to the green road; along the road to Yccen's field; from the field to the hedge-row; along the hedge-row to metsinc [It has been impossible to find a translation for this word. It could be the name of a stream]; along metsinc to the upper part of Ecgerd's hill; along the foot of the hill to the Windrush; along the Windrush to the east part of foul island; along the boundary to Tidreding ford; from there to Occa's slippery place; from there to the southern part of Witta's moor; from there to Collwell Brook; from the valley to the stone bridge; along the brook to the old road; from the road to the boundary of the Hornings; from there to the southern part of the bank; from there along the valley to Tyca's pit; along the brook to the mouth; from the mouth to Ceahha's pond; from there to the little earth mound; from there to the camp to the highest points; from the highest points to Kettle Spring; from the spring to the road; along the road to Hawk's mound; from the mound again to nut cliff where it first began.'

Many of the landmarks mentioned in the charter still exist today, and most of the ways, like Hunter's way, are present-day public footpaths.

When thegn Oelfhelm received his grant from the King, only a small settlement existed on the site of the present town. No archaeological traces have been found, but there are several reasons for thinking that its focus was on Corn Street, where Duck Alley leads into The Crofts. Duck Alley used to be part of a footpath, now blocked off, which led from the Windrush through the present-day West Oxfordshire College grounds and across Corn Street. The river end of the footpath is near Early's blanket factory, and the first recorded name for a mill on this site was Woodford Mill, showing that there was a ford near the mill. Rev Dr J.H. Giles, in his *History of Witney* suggests that there was a north-south Roman road. If this is so (and it must be admitted that there is no evidence), it would have formed a crossroads with the east-west route from the Windrush at Cogges to Corn Street, or Corndell, as it was first recorded.

If Corn Street was indeed the centre of an early Saxon village, there would have been some form of church nearby. This could well have been on the site of 45 Corn Street, a property belonging to the Charity Commissioners. There is no knowing how it became a charity property, as its first records only go back to 1640, though the donors of all the other charity properties of that date are known. Giles suggests that there was an ecclesiastical building on the land that had long since been pulled down. This may well be the site of the earliest church in the town.

The last piece of evidence in the search for a Saxon settlement concerns an important change in ownership of the 30 hides at Wyttenige, nearly 80 years after Oelfhelm received them. Evidently the land had reverted to Royal control for, in 1044, King Edward the Confessor signed a charter very like the earlier one, granting it to Alfwine, Bishop of Winchester. From then onwards the Bishop and his successors developed the town according to their own plans. It is more likely that they built a new church and palace outside the existing settlement, rather than on top of it; and later, when they came to lay out a new market place, it would have been alongside the old settlement.

Edward the Confessor's mother was one of the witnesses who signed the charter in 1044. She was Queen Emma, whose name is commemorated in a modern Witney street name, though her links with the town are tantalisingly hard to trace. In their histories of Witney both Monk and Giles mention, with some scepticism, the idea that she had local connections.

The theory comes from two sources: firstly from the name Em's Ditch, and secondly from the presence of her signature on the charter. The charter mentions as one of the boundary marks a newly-cut ditch which could have been part of Em's Ditch. There is no evidence that this landmark was ever called Emma's Ditch: it was either Em's or Ham's. The Queen's name certainly appears on the charter, but so do those of at least ten members of the King's court, so not much importance can be attached to that. However, the story of Queen Emma has become so much a part of the folklore of Witney that it is worth looking at in some detail.

She was a Norman princess who came over to England to marry Ethelred the Unready, by whom she had two sons, Edward and Alfred. After her husband's death in 1016 the country was ruled by the Danes under King Canute (1016-1035), who married the widowed Emma. Their son Hardicanute reigned briefly after Canute's death, and in 1042 Emma's eldest son, whom we know as Edward the Confessor, came to the throne. Emma's place in national history must surely be secure, for she was married to two kings and mother to two others.

Legend has it that the Archbishop of Canterbury accused Queen Emma of undue intimacy with the Bishop of Winchester, whose connection with Witney was well established under the charter. To prove her innocence, the intrepid Queen is said to have volunteered to undergo an ordeal of fire in Winchester Cathedral. Blindfold, she was made to walk among nine red-hot ploughshares, but emerged triumphantly unhurt. To celebrate this public restoration of her honour, she gave nine manors to the Church of Winchester.

It is an intriguing story but a doubtful one, unsupported by reliable evidence, and made even more unlikely by the fact that at the time it could have happened, the Queen was well over sixty years old. In spite of the story's lack of credibility, she is pleasantly remembered in the street called Queen Emma's Dyke. After all, we may have no proof that she ever visited the town - but proof that she stayed away is equally lacking.

The next piece of evidence of Witney's beginnings is found in the Domesday survey of 1086. That stated that Witney (or Witenie) was still held by the Bishop of Winchester. There were 30 hides (a hide by this time had become a unit of taxation rather than a measure of area), and land for 23 ploughs. '. . . there is now in his lordship [the Bishop's] 5 ploughs. There are 9 bondsmen, 36 townsmen, and 11 borderers having 20 ploughs. There are 2 mills of 32 shillings and 6 pence. The wood 3 leagues long and 2 leagues broad, 4 acres of meadow. In King Edward's time the whole was valued at 22 pounds, now at 25 pounds.'

The bondsmen, townsmen and borderers mentioned in the Domesday survey add up to 56 people so, if we assume that most of them had families, it is probable that there was a population of about 280 people at the time. The two mills were on the sites of what are now Farm Mill and Witney Mill. They were more likely to have been corn than fulling mills; the first written evidence for fulling mills in England comes much later, in 1185, when one is recorded on the Windrush, near Temple Guiting, and another at Newsham in Yorkshire. It is not until 1223 that records show a fulling mill in Witney.

It was probably Stigand, Bishop of Winchester from 1047-1070, who began the building of a palace next to the church. Archaeological evidence suggests that it consisted of a large, rectangular solar tower, which served as private quarters for the owner, a hall and a chapel. These early buildings were constantly embellished and improved over the next century. A latrine block was added to the solar. A gate-house and out-buildings were constructed. The Bishop's Pipe Rolls mention a hall with a louvre (a dome-shaped opening in the roof to allow the smoke to escape), a chapel 'next to a room of the monks', a wardrobe, a kitchen, a pantry, a store-room, a buttery, stable and cellar.

Sometime between 1135 and 1150, the period of the Civil War between King Stephen and Matilda, it was found necessary to fortify the palace. This was done by piling earth round the outside walls so that a large mound was formed up to the first floor, which became the new ground floor: the ground floor became a cellar. The Bishop who ordered the fortification was Henry of Blois, Bishop of Winchester from 1129 until his death in 1171. He was the brother of King Stephen himself, and certainly the most powerful man in England, if not in Europe. Henry of Blois was Stephen's most influential supporter in his struggle for the throne. He had hoped that Stephen would show his gratitude by appointing him Archbishop of Canterbury when the position became vacant in 1139: he could then have emulated his predecessor Bishop Stigand, who had held both sees. When Stephen failed to grant his brother's wishes, Henry transferred his loyalty to Empress Matilda. Given the complexity of his political life, it is understandable that Henry needed to fortify his palace - even if it was just one of many residences. We do not know how often he visited it, or whether the fortifications were ever put to the test.

The next major - and exciting - development in Witney took place under Peter des Roches, Bishop of Winchester (1205-1238). It was he who laid out the town as it is today; he was a property developer with a good head for business. He set up a large triangular market-place running northwards from the church, with long narrow plots of land at right angles. These narrow strips of land - called burgage plots - are still the dividing lines between some present-day properties.

Before Witney was laid out as a market town, the main route from the north east crossed the Windrush near the old moated manor house at Cogges, and followed Crown Lane (Langdale Gate) to the centre of the town. When the new market place was set up, the approach road was changed to the present one, and a bridge was built over the Windrush on the site of to-day's two-arched structure.

The exact date of the laying-out of Witney's market is uncertain, but a reference in the Bishop of Winchester's account rolls for the year 1208-9, gives permission for licence to lease land for building on newly-cleared ground. The second decade of the 13th century was the heyday of speculative development and across the Windrush at Cogges, lord of the manor Robert d'Arsic essayed a new settlement of 32 two-acre holdings. This is the area known today as Newland. The same thing was happening in Eynsham, where the Abbot of Eynsham Abbey laid out a new market at Newlands.

During the 13th century Witney must have been a prosperous place. We know that the cloth-making industry had already started, for back in 1179 records show that a weaver was fined 6s 8d for selling inferior cloth, and in 1223 a fulling mill is recorded. The Bishop's Palace, with its resident dignitaries, must have been an important element in the growth of the new town. There were even visits from royalty. That far from popular monarch, King John, came to Witney on several occasions between 1207 and 1214, probably from his palace at Woodstock or his hunting lodge at Langley. These visits from the King and the Bishop, with their retinues, must have been a powerful stimulus to local trade. In 1221 the 14-year-old Henry III came to stay with Bishop Peter des Roches in Witney, and spent the considerable sum of £20 on new clothes for the royal wardrobe. In 1231 the same King granted the right for a second fair to be held in Witney: the first had been granted in 1202. By 1220 the Borough was important enough to be assessed for tax on its own account, rather than as part of the manor, which remained responsible for taxes on the farmland surrounding the Borough.

The Bishop encouraged people to move into his new town by granting them certain privileges, including the right to be quit of toll, passage money and murage (a tax levied for the building or repairing of the walls of a town).

By 1279 Witney consisted of over 300 messuages, or plots, and in the Hundred Rolls of that year the inquisition, as the inspectors were called, found that there were 226 holders of messuages, 30 of them women, and 56 were wealthy enough to hold more than one messuage. This suggests that, by the end of the 13th century, the population of Witney was something more than a thousand inhabitants.

In 1250 the Bishop made some more improvements. He laid out a deer park in the wood of Warfordsleigh on the hill opposite the town: this is to the west of what is now Windrush Valley Estate, or Smith's Estate, as many people call it, after the company that set it up. Henry III sent an order to his keeper of Wychwood Forest to give to the Bishop '20 acres of timber, 15 live does, and 5 live bucks to stock the park at Witney'. The park was surrounded by a stone wall. In the Bishop's accounts there is an entry in 1285 for lime and stone to build 231 perches of park wall at the cost of £25 18s 5d. The park itself remained as a recognisable enclosure well into the 17th century. Today a small part of the wall can be seen between the bicycle track and the old A40 to the west of the town. The name of Deer Park Road commemorates the park.

The second half of the 12th century brought a rapid expansion of population. Settlements grew, and towns flourished. Witney was no exception. During the latter half of the 13th and the early part of the 14th century it must have been a busy and thriving community, sending two burgesses to meet the Lords in Parliament at Westminster. However, as the main purpose of the Parliament was to vote the King money, there was little advantage to the townspeople. In 1360 the burgesses petitioned to be released from the privilege.

The Hundred Rolls of 1278 say that Witney had a wealthy market on Thursdays and two fairs. It still has a Thursday market (wealthy or not), though it no longer sells livestock. It is probable that some time in the 13th century two more market places were laid out, one in Corndell, now called Corn Street, and the other at West End.

The name West End seems puzzling, as it is on the north east side of Witney: the explanation is that the area was originally part of the parish of Hailey, not Witney.

In 1348 came catastrophe in the form of the Black Death, which raged through Europe and the British Isles. Up to a third of the local population died of bubonic plague during 1348 and 1349.

The effects of the plague on the Bishop's farming were dramatic and disastrous. He was no longer able to depend on serf labour to reap his harvest. The profit per acre fell from 2s 5d in the years before 1349 to 3d for the following five years. In 1348 the Bishop had 53 virgaters working at harvest time: these workers were unpaid. In 1349 the number had fallen to 21, and in 1353 only six were working for him. The expenses of running the estate went up from £25 in 1348 to £866 in 1352. After the plague the Bishop leased out far more of his land, and cultivated far less for himself; the Black Death had brought an end to the feudal system as far as labour service was concerned, and it was now more lucrative to live off rents.

The Bishops of Winchester continued to have a connection with the manor and the Borough until the middle of the nineteenth century. There were two short periods when they lost control of the manor. During the reign of Edward VI, when Bishop John Ponet, a Protestant Bishop who had replaced the Catholic Bishop Gardiner, relinquished his lands to the Crown in 1551, he received an annuity. This was a time when the Crown was making a determined effort to lay its hands on as much church land as possible. Sir Andrew Dudley, brother to the Duke of Northumberland, was granted the manor and Borough of Witney. Dudley was not able to enjoy the income from them for long, for in 1553 Mary came to the throne and the Catholic Bishop Gardiner was restored as Bishop of Winchester, though the lands were not returned until 1558. During the Commonwealth (1647) the Bishops again lost title to their estates, and William Lenthall, Speaker in the Long Parliament, became lord of the manor. At the Restoration they once more regained their estates. From the end of the 14th century much of the manorial land had been let out to yeoman families. The Brices leased the manor during the 16th and early 17th centuries. After the Restoration the lease passed from a local family to powerful lords. In 1670 Lord Cornbury was lessee, followed by the Earl of Clarendon and then the Earl of Rochester. The Duke of Marlborough bought the lease in 1751 and purchased the manor in 1862, so bringing an end to the Winchester connection.

Pottery found at the bottom of the Bishop's Palace garderobe (latrine). (OAU)

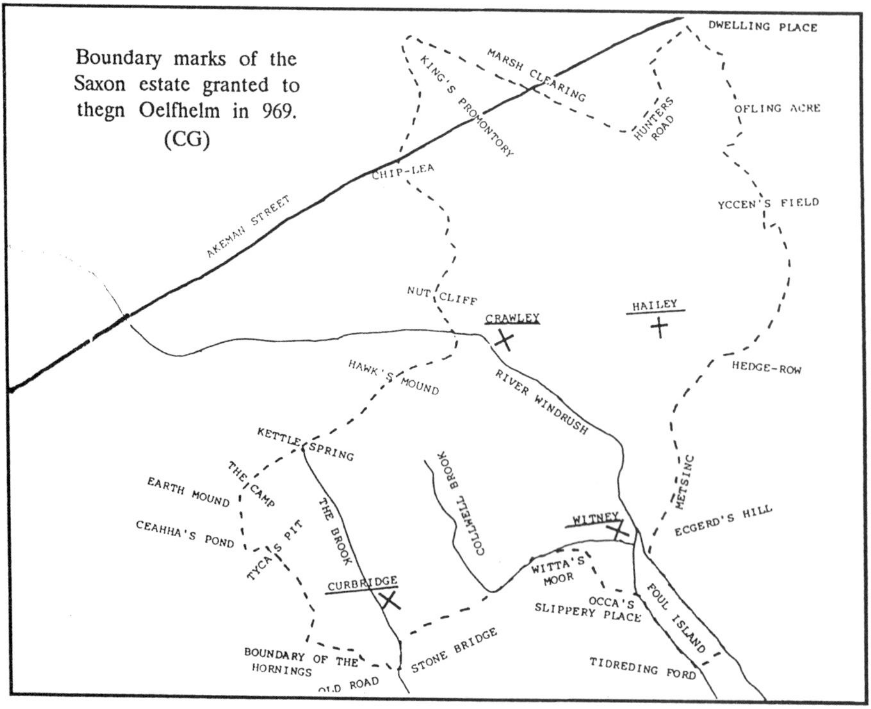

Boundary marks of the Saxon estate granted to thegn Oelfhelm in 969. (CG)

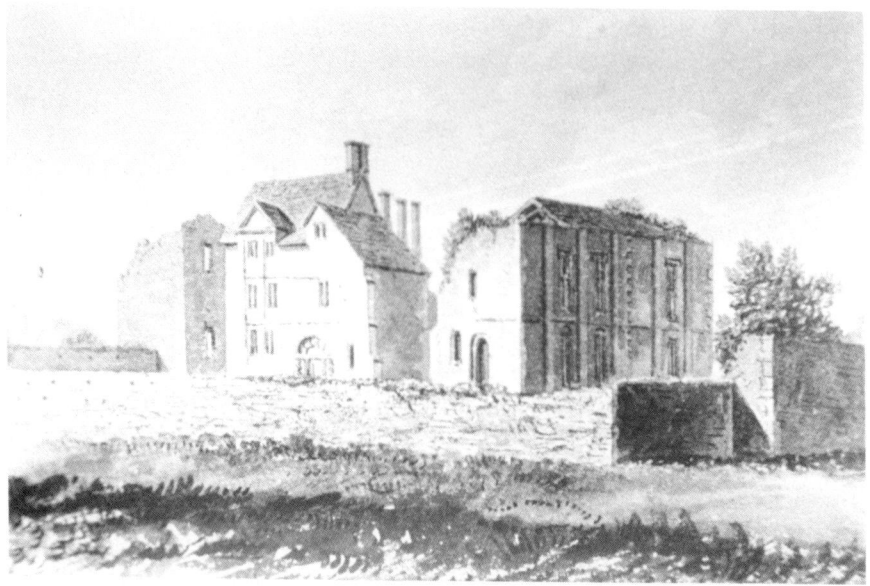

The Bishop's Palace, from a pen and ink drawing c1729, attributed to Nathaniel Buck. (BL: Gough Maps, 26, f60)

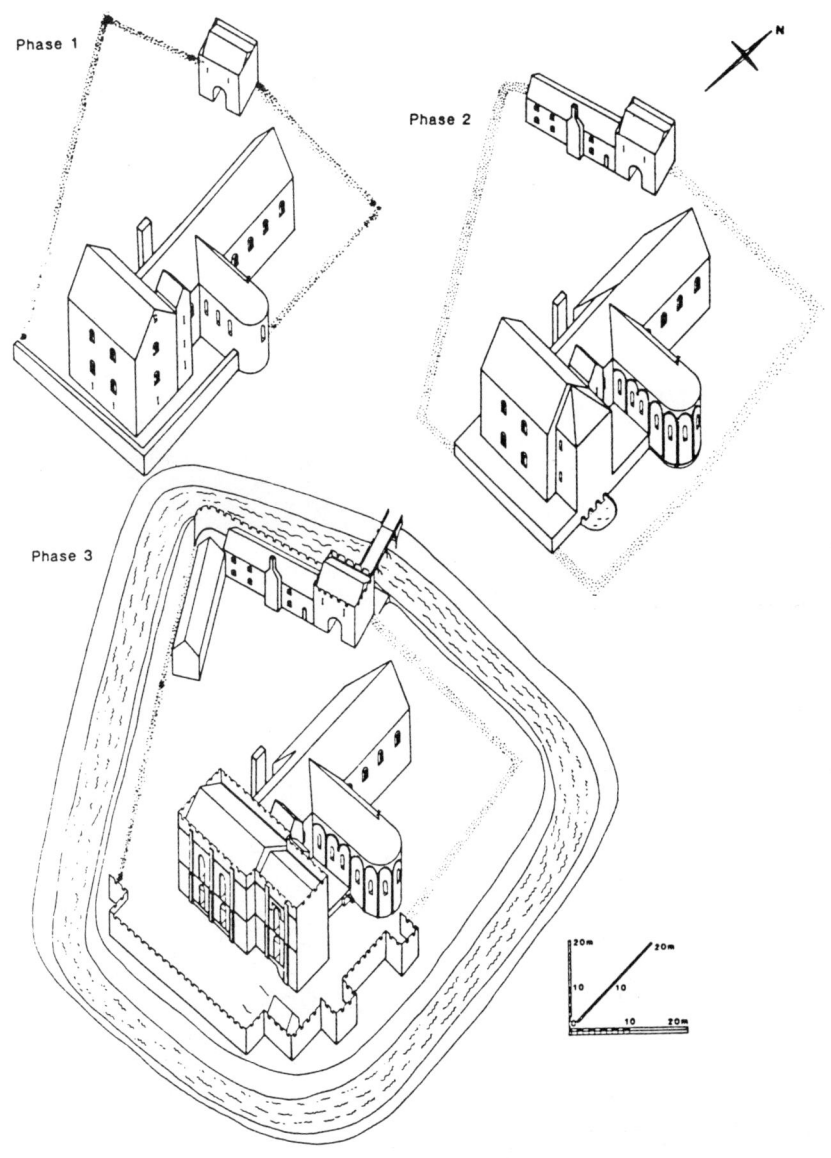

Phases of building the palace. (OAU)

LEFT: The culvert leading to the moat at the bottom of the latrines. These loos were probably used by King John when he visited Witney between 1207 and 1214.
RIGHT: Part of the stonework, looking as fresh as when it was built — though there is some graffiti carved on it. (OAU)

Building which used to stand in Duck Alley, drawn by W. Seely, 1832. No 53 Corn Street is on the corner of this old alley.

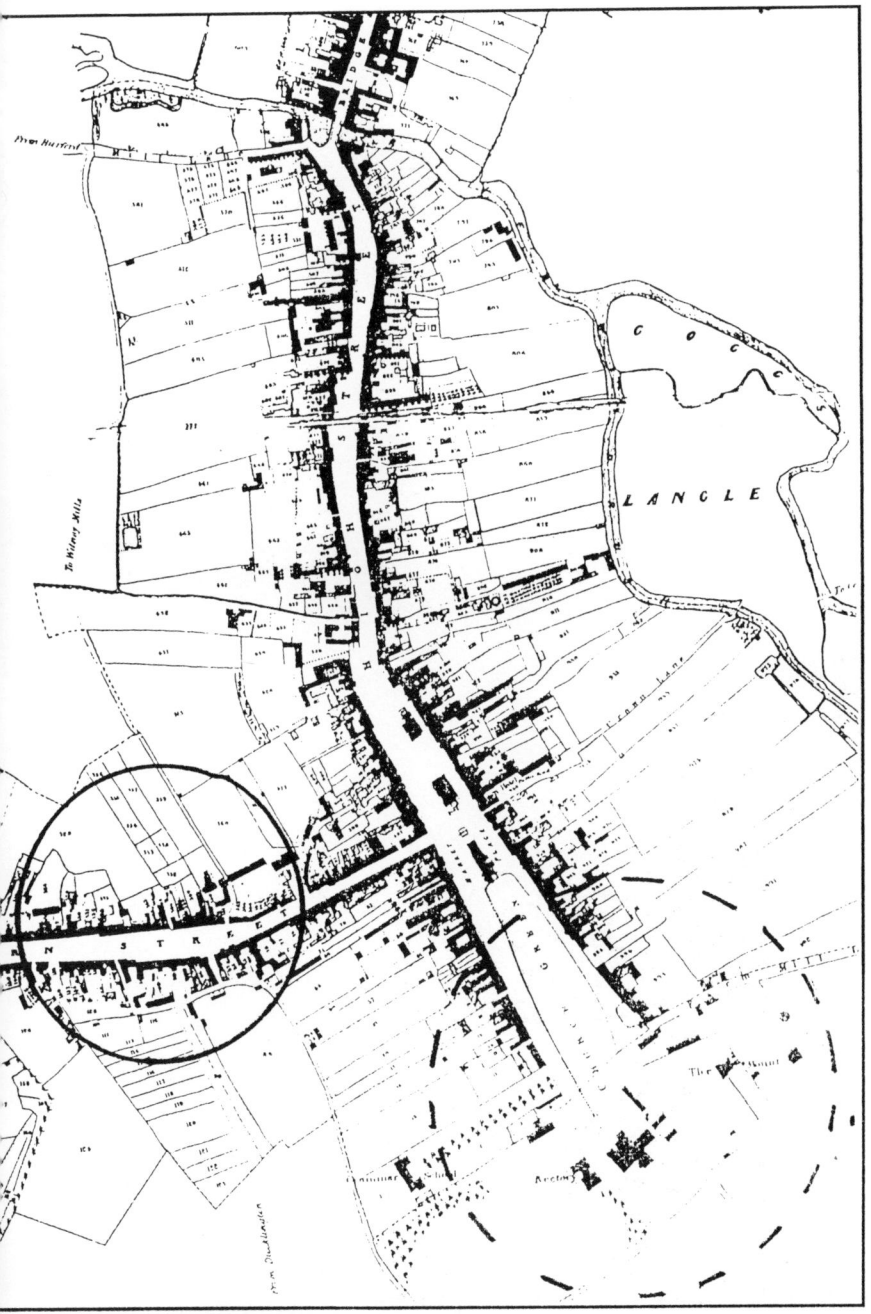

Possible extent of Saxon settlement. ——————
Possible extent of settlement in the C12. - - - - - - -

The Church with John Holloway's Almshouses which were rebuilt to the design of William Wilkinson in 1868.

Bread and beef cottages. (CG)

THE POOR ARE ALWAYS WITH US

Before the dissolution of monastic houses, the church had borne the main burden of looking after the poor and needy, whose numbers were high in times of bad harvests, high wheat prices or plague. After dissolution, new systems of support had to be devised.

This support centred on the parish, which was required, by a series of Poor Laws at the end of the 16th century, to raise a rate for the benefit of the poor. This parish relief was supplemented by money bequeathed by wealthy parishioners.

In Tudor times Witney, with its many prosperous wool merchants, was quite a wealthy place. In consequence the town was well endowed with charities for the relief of its poor.

The most important became known as the 'Freeland Charity' because its money was invested in land at Freeland in the parish of Eynsham. It is first recorded in 1652, though it is certainly older than that. In 1652, and again in 1682, commissions were set up to examine the state of charities throughout the county, to see that they were being properly administered, and that the money was used for the purpose intended by the testators.

When the Commissioners visited Witney in September 1682, they found that £417 10s 0d had been left by various people for the relief of the poor: Richard Ashcombe of Curbridge £100; George Tomson of Bampton £30; Stephen Brice £40; Thomas Sheppard of Bampton £8; William Edgerley £10; Elizabeth Sharpe £2; Hugh Barker DD £30; 'One Bolt of Oxford' £5; A person unknown £1 10s; John Martin of Witney Esq £5; Elizabeth Green of Shipton £16; Henry James of Castleton £20; John Palmer of Bampton £50; Philip Box £30; ---- Fifield £20 and Edward Carter of Alvescot £50, totalling £417 10s 0d.

Most of this money was given at the end of the 16th century. Richard Ashcombe died in 1606. He was a wealthy landowner and wool merchant, who owned Witney Farm in Curbridge and Holway Grange. In his will he was able to leave his wife £800 'in a little black trunk with a padlock on in my chamber in Witney'. George Tomson of Bampton owned moveable property worth £951 when he died in 1603. Besides leaving £30 to the poor of Witney, he also left money to the poor of Burford and Bampton. The Brice family were weavers in the town during the 15th century, and Stephen leased the manor and the Borough from the Bishops of Winchester. The family remained lessees of the Borough until the 17th century. Philip Box, who contributed £30, was the grandfather of Henry Box, founder of the Grammar School. Philip Box was Bailiff of Witney in 1573 and Churchwarden in 1571 and 1573. The £1 10s from a person unknown was probably the 30s given to the use of the town of Witney in the year 1600 by 'Mr John Attwell, parson, of Cornwall, to the use of the poor artificers and craftsmen of the borough'. This same sum of money is again referred to in the Witney court book of 1609 as being 'the gift of a parson in Devonshire'. It has been impossible to trace the other benefactors, but all the surnames are those of prominent Witney families of the 16th century.

As a result of the Charity Commissioners' visit in 1682, this £417 10s 0d, along with a further £64 10s 0d 'being money belonging to the town of Witney', was used to purchase an estate called Threfts in Freeland, Eynsham. This land was let, and the income from the rent used to help support the poor.

During the 18th century most of the money went to providing apprentices' indenture fees. At the time it was common practice for a master, when taking on an apprentice, to receive a fee of £5 (by the end of the 18th century it had risen to £10). All but one of the apprentices whose indenture fee was paid by the charity were boys. The exception was Martha Breakspear, apprenticed in 1698 to Thomas Parmo, a fellmonger, to learn household employment.

While most of the boys were apprenticed to blanket weavers and allied trades, such as fulling and dyeing, some were employed in more unusual occupations. There were apprentice cordwainers, basket makers and blacksmiths. Joseph Early, son of Thomas Early, was in 1790 apprenticed to Thomas Savory of Oxford as a plumber and glazier. Other boys trained as tailors, shoemakers, harnessmakers, breechesmakers and chimney sweeps. Most of the Witney lads were apprenticed in the town, but there were some who were sent to the surrounding towns, and others to London or even further afield. In the 1790s James Cork was sent to Hereford to learn to be a shoemaker, and in 1807 James Haynes was apprenticed to James Tyrie of Little Queen Street, St Giles-in-the-Field, Middlesex, as a coach joiner.

Over 350 indenture certificates dating from 1670 to 1820 have survived in the Witney parish chest, as receipts for the money that the charity paid out. However, these payments stopped in about 1822. This was not because the system had come to an end, but because Witney had had another visit from the Charity Commissioners, who were not happy about the way the charity was spending its income. They found that it was not only the poor and needy whose fees were paid, but anybody who applied. There were many cases of sons being apprenticed to their fathers, and the fathers getting the fee.

After 1822 most of the Freeland charity money was spent on bread and beef for the poor at Christmas. By the end of the 19th century this distribution of Christmas cheer had got somewhat out of hand, and was causing concern among responsible citizens. Throughout the 1890s there were repeated demands at vestry meetings to see the accounts, but they fell on deaf ears. There were also letters in the *Witney Gazette* demanding reform. On 23 July 1910 the Charity Commissioners again visited Witney, and again did not like what they saw. Could there really be 2,330 people in Witney in need of Christmas handouts? Could families in receipt of over £1 a week truly be called poor? In 1909, 2,609lbs of beef had been given away at Christmas, costing £105, and £14 worth of bread had been distributed.

There was a considerable outcry when the Commissioners put a stop to the large-scale distribution of bread and beef which many of the inhabitants felt was theirs by right, in spite of the fact that the churchwardens, who divided up the meat, would often find joints outside their doors, left by disgruntled townsfolk who felt their families were entitled to cuts of better quality.

A further scandal was revealed when the Commissioners went through the accounts of the Freeland charity. Why had no rents been received lately for the shooting rights on the Freeland estate? Before 1900 a small income had been so derived. The explanation was simple: the trustees had been enjoying free shooting. That was the position in 1910. The Charity Commissioners then recommended that the Freeland charity and all the other small charities for the town's poor be combined, so that they could be better administered and the needy more adequately catered for.

Charities were unable to support the vast majority of the poor, so it fell to the parish rate to provide food, clothing and shelter for those who could not keep themselves. The parishioners of Witney, like ratepayers everywhere, disliked having to dig too deeply into their pockets, so every effort was made to keep the poor rate as low as possible. This tended to mean that the conditions in the Workhouse were uncomfortable enough to discourage people from applying for parish relief, though the workhouses of the 18th century were not nearly such unpleasant places as the union workhouses of the next century. The first known mention of a workhouse in Witney is in 1747.

During the 17th century, the poor were kept in the Bridewell with the petty criminals. The name Bridewell came from the Royal lodging near Saint Bride's Well in the City of London, which was given by Edward IV for a hospital and later converted into a house of correction. In the early part of the century the City of Oxford sent offenders to the Bridewell in Witney, and paid the Witney Vestry to look after them.

In 1747, when the overseers found that 'the poor of the parish of Witney are becoming very numerous', and that 'the idle poor who are well able to work have taken to charity which should have been paid to the aged and infirm who are the real object of charity and compassion', they decided to establish a workhouse, with the accent very much on work. The overseers and churchwardens appointed Edward Bolton, baker, of Witney, to provide 'meat and drink, washing lodging and apparel for the poor', and paid him £230 for three years. In exchange for their keep the Workhouse inmates had to work hard and hand over their earnings to the Workhouse keeper. In this way, by paying someone to look after the able-bodied poor, the parish was able to keep down its rates. This move was sanctioned by the Workhouse Act of 1722, which allowed the contracting out of workhouses, the contractor's function being 'to keep, maintain and employ the poor and taking benefit of their work for maintenance'.

In 1810 the Vestry minutes record that 'Mr Daniel Hartshorn has agreed to take the poor of the parish to maintain and clothe them for £1480'. This Workhouse was 45 Corn Street, which originally consisted of three cottages and a garden that belonged to the town's charities. They were enlarged by means of a loan from Robert Collier and John Clinch. The Master of the Workhouse sometimes held street collections. William Gardener, who was born in 1813 and died in 1906, remembered seeing 'the Master of the Corn Street Workhouse, accompanied by the inmates, wheeling a barrow through the streets with a huge box as a receptacle for the coppers which he collected for the poor rate'. The old cottages that formed this early workhouse were much altered in Victorian times and part became the premises of Thomas Cook, coach and carriage builder.

The last decade of the 18th century saw a vast increase in the price of wheat. It rose from 50s a quarter in the early 1790s to 88s in 1796, and by 1800 had reached the unheard-of sum of 130s. This enormous increase was caused by a series of poor harvests, and had a dramatic effect on the amount of money that the parish had to provide for relief. In 1794 £820 was spent; by the turn of the century this had risen to £2,837, and a peak of £3,197 was reached in 1820. The Vestry did all in its power to keep the poor rate to a minimum. Tenders were entered into for the supply of food to the Workhouse: 'Thomas Diver agreed to provide a sufficient quantity of bacon at 10d per lb and best assorted potatoes at 3s per sack'. Likewise, Richard Spittle was 'to provide a sufficient quantity of good wheaten bread at 20d per half peck loaf'. All the costs of the Workhouse were scrutinised monthly by an inspector appointed by the Vestry.

At this time of inflated wheat prices the vast increase in the number of people living below the breadline meant that a new workhouse was called for. In order to keep the parish rate down, a union workhouse was established, combining the parishes of Witney, Curbridge, Hailey and Cogges. Such combined workhouses were sanctioned under Gilbert's Act of 1782. In 1836 it was built to a design of George Wilkinson of Witney. This imposing building occupied the site on Tower Hill which now accommodates the firm of Crawford Collets, and was partly demolished in 1978.

More agreeable accommodation took the form of almshouses. Witney has three sets of these, two of which are on Church Green. The ones actually in the churchyard were originally endowed by John Holloway, the philanthropist who founded the Blue Coat School. In his will of 1723 he directed his executors, within five years of his decease, 'to cause an almshouse to be built, on Church Green, for the residence of six poor widows'. Each house was to have 'a lower and an upper room, together with a little garden, and other things necessary'. The original almshouses no longer exist: they were rebuilt to the design of William Wilkinson in 1868.

The other almshouses on Church Green, near the entrance to Henry Box School, date back to Tudor times. They are first mentioned in an inquisition taken by the Commission of Charitable Uses in 1652. 'There was belonging to and for the use of the poor people of Witney, an almshouse and a garden, in Witney consisting of three several parts and tenements, in which poor and indigent people of the borough of Witney were placed, and did inhabit.' By the end of the 18th century these almshouses were described as 'being in a wretched state of repair and unfit for habitation'. The old houses were pulled down, and 'six new substantial tenements of two storeys, were built at the expense of £354'. They were further modernised in 1814, with the addition of a kitchen and a fuel store at the back. These cottages, strictly speaking, ceased to be almshouses, and were let for rent. After the money that had been spent on their modernisation had been repaid, the income from the rents was used to help the poor. This help was mainly in the form of bread and beef at Christmas, and so the cottages came to be known as the 'bread and beef houses'.

The third set of almshouses, near Staple Hall, was founded by William Townsend in 1821 for six aged unmarried women. The Townsend family had been well-known in Witney for many generations, and kept the Staple Hall Inn during the 17th century. At the time he founded the almshouses, William Townsend had left Witney and become a haberdasher in London.

William Wilkinson's Gothic style rebuilding of Holloway's almshouses. (JG)

Church Green. The 'bread and beef houses' are the small cottages at the end of the row. W. Seely 1856.

William Townsend's almshouses for six aged unmarried women, built 1821. (CG)

The Old Blanket Market, Witney 1870

The Butter Cross. In 1606 Richard Ashcombe left £50 to build 'a house over and above the Cross.' The clock was added later, after a bequest from William Blake of Cogges in 1683. The centre pillar is possibly the base of an old market cross, though tradition has it that a statue of the Virgin stood on the spot.

BOX AND BLUECOAT

The most prestigious school in Witney during the 17th and 18th centuries was the Grammar School founded by Henry Box in 1660. Henry Box was born in 1585 of a Witney family. He studied at Oriel College, Oxford, later becoming a prosperous businessman in London and a prominent member of the Grocers' Company. Wishing to do something for his home town, the elderly Henry Box decided to emulate many other philanthropists of his time, and to endow a grammar school. He bought some land beside the Rectory, and had a school built on it in 1660. This attractive and well-proportioned building is still in use; the school has been extended several times in its long life, but the original schoolhouse remains the focal point for the passer-by on Church Green.

Henry Box himself died only two years after founding the school, but his widow and sole executrix, Mary, took over all the arrangements. Upkeep was provided by a rent charge of £50 per annum from property in Longworth. A formal Act in 1663 said that the four Wardens of the Grocers' Company were to be Governors, and that the Provost and four senior Fellows of Oriel would be Visitors, coming to the school annually on 25 July (St James's day). The teaching would be entrusted to a Master and an Usher. The qualifications and duties of these two pedagogues were strictly defined by Mary Box in the 'Statutes Constitutions Orders and Directions' of the school: as one would expect, they had to be of the highest moral and religious character. As for academic qualifications, the Master was required to be an MA and the Usher a graduate if possible. They concentrated on Latin, Greek and Hebrew. The more prosaic skills of writing and arithmetic were taken care of by a 'wrighting master', who did not live in, as the Master and Usher did.

There was one essential qualification for the pupils: they had to be able to read English perfectly. They were divided into foundationers and foreigners. The foundationers formed a privileged group of 30 boys, drawn both from Witney town and from descendants of the Box family. They received free tuition. The rest of the pupils were 'foreigners' from further afield, whose parents paid fees set by the Master and Usher.

Between 1663 and 1767 the Masters were mostly distinguished academics and clergymen, respected by the townspeople as well as by their hardworking pupils. There was unfortunately one, John Goole, BA, whose long reign was a disaster. In spite of plummeting numbers and accusations of neglect, irresponsibility, excessive beating and anti-Dissenter discrimination, he managed to remain in power for 39 years - until his death, in fact. The next Master was able to revive the school, which continued quite successfully until he retired in 1767. After that there was a long period of decline, a fate shared by a great many of the grammar schools in the 18th and 19th centuries, when a more utilitarian form of education, with the emphasis on the 'three R's', became popular, and when schools were being opened to cater for various dissenting religious groups. For years attendance at the Grammar School failed to reach double figures, and in May 1839 there was a Master but not a single pupil.

In 1877, after years of varying fortunes, the school was re-classified, on the recommendation of the Charity Commissioners, as a 'Second Grade' or 'Middle-Class' school to cater for boys without university aspirations. They were to study English subjects, arithmetic, mathematics, natural science, French, Latin, drawing, vocal music, book-keeping and various extras. In this form the school settled into a period of calm stability, though numbers (never more than 28) were disappointing.

Meanwhile, scientific and technical education was gaining in importance everywhere. In 1898 a Technical School was opened in Witney, and it soon became clear to the Grocers' Company and the County Council that it would be sensible to amalgamate it with the Grammar School. This process was completed in 1902. The Grocers' Company, which had faithfully and generously carried out Henry Box's wishes for 240 years in good times and bad, handed over responsibility to the County, though it continued to contribute £100 a year to the school and take a benevolent interest in its progress.

At the same time the Blue Coat School, founded by John Holloway in 1723, was closed down and the endowment used for scholarships to the new Witney Grammar and Technical School, as well as for other educational purposes in the spirit of the Holloway charity.

The Technical School had been open to girls as well as boys, so they became entitled to go to the new foundation. By 1905 there were two women teachers on the staff, and by 1911 about half the pupils were girls. The school prospered steadily from the time of the amalgamation, though it was inconvenient for pupils to commute between the Old Block for Arts subjects and the Technical Institute in the High Street for Science. By 1910 a New Block had been opened to solve this problem and cater for ever-increasing numbers.

In 1922 the school became known once more as Witney Grammar School. Academic and sporting successes became more and more frequent; many boys and girls went on to universities and gained good degrees.

The school's tercentenary year was 1960, culminating in a visit from Queen Elizabeth the Queen Mother. She arrived by helicopter on 20 July, and spent the afternoon at the school, opening some splendid new buildings and attending a lunch and a garden party.

More changes were on the way, however, for later in the 1960s grammar schools were phased out in Oxfordshire. The school became Comprehensive in 1969, and reverted to the name of its original founder, Henry Box, who would surely be gratified if he could see the building he planned looking as good as new, and surrounded by attractive modern extensions, providing space for 1,000 pupils.

In 1953 a big new school was opened at Wood Green, with up-to-date facilities and large playing-fields. It started life as a Secondary Modern school, but became Comprehensive in 1968. Though its tercentenary may be a long way off, it has celebrated its Silver Jubilee. It has acquired a Sixth Form block and purpose-built accommodation for all kinds of educational and sporting activities. More playing fields have been purchased, and the swimming pool is one of the attractions of a school which has become known for its sound academic results and enterprising out-of-school activities. At present, Wood Green caters for about the same number of pupils as its more venerable counterpart.

Sixty years after Henry Box's death, Thomas Early (1655-1733), a blanket weaver and from 1703 a bailiff of the town, persuaded John Holloway, a wealthy cloth merchant with land and property in Witney and Hailey, to leave money to found a school more suited to the times. Holloway did more: in 1723 he left his house on Narrow Hill to be used as a schoolhouse. The endowment for the school came from his land in Stonesfield and in Hailey.

In his will John Holloway stated that the school was to be for the sons of poor journeymen weavers, and that the pupils should be clothed 'in the manner of the Bluecoat Hospital boys in London'. A Nonconformist and no lover of the established church, Holloway further directed that the schoolmaster 'should be no clergyman but a very sober man and a good scrivener who can cast accounts . . . for doing so he shall have the sum of £10 per annum paid twice yearly.'

The Blue Coat School aimed to educate, clothe and feed 15 boys: ten from Witney and five from Hailey. They started at seven years old, and stayed until they were 14, when the school paid their indenture fees to allow them to become apprentices in the blanket industry. As a result of a recommendation of the Charity Commissioners in 1822, the school was opened up to the sons of other operatives in the industry as well as weavers. John Wright, a Witney man living in America, added £4,800 to its funds in 1860.

With the reorganisation of educational establishments in Witney in 1902, the Blue Coat School and its charities were amalgamated with the Grammar School. Its 24 pupils left the building, which then became the West End elementary school, for it was considered too far for the younger children to walk from West End to St Mary's School on Church Green.

At the beginning of the 18th century there were no charity schools in Witney, according to the Rector's return to the Bishop of Oxford in 1738. The Rector, Robert Freind, goes on to say that he himself started a charity school for 12 boys 'who were clothed and taught to read and write at my expense'; he carried on this school for six years, in the hope 'that I might by degrees have drawn in the parish to joyn with me in that design'. The Rector did not run the school in person, but paid someone to teach the boys. In fact, by his own admission, he only lived in Witney for five months of the year, and some of this time was spent in the City of Bath for his health's sake.

The third charity school was endowed in 1695 under the will of William Blake, Lord of the Manor of Cogges, who also endowed schools at High Cogges and Newland. This school, in the High Street, was run by a schoolmistress who lived in the house rent-free, and received £6 a year for instructing 30 children between the ages of six and nine. The 'poor schoolmistress' was to be paid once a year at Michaelmas, but often her 'pay cheque' was late, as the money came out of the rents of an estate left for this purpose, and the tenants frequently failed to pay on time. She was able to make some extra income by charging for children under six years of age. This school seems to have disappeared in the middle of the 19th century. It was flourishing in 1822 when the Charity Commissioners inspected the charity schools of the area, but it is not mentioned in their records of the 1870s.

As well as these charity schools there were many privately run schools. Most of them sprang up, existed for a few years and then vanished, usually without trace.

At the beginning of the 19th century the Church took an active role in promoting education, with the founding of the National School Movement. In 1813 the Movement called a meeting in the Blanket Hall, and it was decided to found a National School on Bridge Street. This later moved to Church Green. William Smith, who grew up to play an important part in Witney's industrial and social history, went there in the early 1820s, but considered it 'humble fare' compared with the Blue Coat School.

The National School charged a penny a week. Reading, writing and arithmetic were taught, and of course religious instruction was an important subject. In 1838 an infants' school was added, holding its classes in the Wenman Chapel in the Church. By the end of the 19th century, when the National School was taken over by the newly-formed County Council, it had accommodation for 450 children, and an average attendance of 140 boys and 150 girls.

Nonconformists have played an important part in establishing local schools. A Quaker schoolroom was built in about 1698, and continued until 1787. The Wesleyans started a mixed school in 1851, though there had been a Wesleyan Sunday school for a long time before that. It was held in an old thatched building, the width of a cottage and 50 feet long, on the north side of the old Chapel. The Sunday School was divided into six classes, and reading and writing were taught. At the turn of the century the school was greatly extended, and became a higher elementary school under the County Council. It was probably the largest elementary school in Oxfordshire; in 1903 it certainly had the highest-paid head teacher in the county, with a salary of £230 a year. No other elementary teacher received more than £200 then.

A crisis arose in the late 1920s: the Church school buildings on Church Green were dilapidated and would cost £2,750 if they were to be repaired and provided with modern heating and sanitation suitable for a junior mixed school. There was also a need for a new senior school, but the cost to the ratepayers would be formidable. The situation was saved by a prominent local family, the Batts, who presented The Hill, a large house in the town centre, to the school trustees. According to the estate agent's booklet the house, set in three acres of ground, had five reception rooms, a full-sized billiard room, 12 bedrooms and dressing-rooms, bathroom, servants' hall and capital stabling. This gift commemorated the family's long connection with the town; for generations doctors by the name of Batt had cared for the sick in Witney. The last of the line, Dr Charles Dorrington Batt, had died at The Hill in 1926. The grateful trustees set about planning a new school to be built in its ample grounds. It was opened in July 1930. By 1964 the Batt School had become a Church of England junior school, and a large extension had been built.

Roman Catholic children came into their own when Our Lady of Lourdes Catholic Primary School was opened in 1959, near the Convent of the Sisters of Charity on Curbridge Road.

Further education came to Witney in the 1950s. It started as a Day Continuation School, and became a Technical College soon afterwards; in 1990 it was re-named the West Oxfordshire College. The Hill, now known as Batt House, was one of the early buildings, and a former mineral water factory was another.

In the late 1960s and early 1970s four large teaching and administrative blocks were built to provide modern classrooms, lecture theatres, sports halls and a library; some of the older buildings are also still in use. Over the years the curriculum has expanded along with the premises. Now, in the 1990s, the College offers numerous full-time courses in, among others, Business, Health Care, Engineering, Computer Studies and Information Technology, as well as GCSE subjects and a highly successful course on the Management of Thoroughbred Horses. In addition, evening classes in a great variety of academic subjects, arts, crafts and hobbies are held, and local societies have meetings in the building. Students come to the West Oxfordshire College from the villages round Witney, and from parts of Gloucestershire and Berkshire, as well as from the town itself.

Witney Grammar School drawn by W. Seely, c1850.

Classroom, Witney Grammar School, c1920 (OCL)

The Grammar School, with the avenue of elm trees, now felled because of Dutch elm disease.

The window on the right is part of the old National School in Bridge Street, founded on the site of the White Hart Inn. Drawn by W. Seely, c1850

Some of the books left to the Grammar School by Henry Box (JG)

The Wesleyan School. (CG)

Jubilee plaque similar to the one high on the wall of the extension to the Wesleyan School. (CG)

Proposed timetable for the Wesleyan School, 1900. (PRO)

Playground of St Mary's School, Church Green. (CG)

WARP AND WEFT

Witney has been famous for the manufacture of blankets for several hundred years, but the origins of the woollen industry are unrecorded. We do know that weavers were at work by the latter half of the 12th century, for a fine of 6s 8d imposed on a weaver of Witney is recorded in the Royal Pipe Rolls of 1179. The fact that young King Henry III spent £20 on clothes in Witney in 1221 suggests that the making of local cloth had reached a high standard.

During the 13th and 14th centuries wool became more and more important here, under the influence of the Bishops of Winchester, who kept ever-increasing flocks of sheep on their demesne land. The Bishop's 1278 account rolls show that 370 sheep were kept, and by 1346 the number had increased to 600; by the end of the 14th century the flock was nearly 1,500 strong.

Before mechanisation began to infiltrate the cloth industry towards the end of the 18th century, most processes were carried out by hand in local houses and cottages. The master weaver, having bought his wool from wool merchants and fellmongers, sorted it according to quality and length of staple, or fibre. He then blended it carefully and added rape oil to make it easier to work. His next step was to load it on to a pack horse and deliver it to families - some local, some many miles away in the Cotswolds - whom he employed to card and spin. The carding was usually done by men and boys, who then handed the combed-out wool over to women, to spin on traditional spinning-wheels. This work was mostly done in the winter, when the men were less busy with their regular jobs as farm workers.

The master weaver collected the pads of spun yarn and made the blankets on his own looms in his house or shed. At this stage they were loose, rough and oily, ready for fulling. This entailed heavy beating of the cloth in large vats containing water and fuller's earth or clay. As the earth was forced through the cloth, the grease was scoured out, and the water caused the blankets to shrink to a firmer texture. The very first fullers (or tuckers, as they are often called) are thought to have used their feet to pound the cloth, but from an early stage this was done in special fulling mills, using river water both for power and for the cleansing process: the first definite record of a fulling mill on the Windrush at Witney appears in 1223. It may have been there for a considerable time before that; they were known in Oxfordshire at the end of the 12th century. There is a record of one at Barford in 1185 and another at Brightwell in 1208. By the end of the 14th century there were two such mills in Witney.

After the fulling process, the nap was raised on the cloth by means of teazles, and the blankets were stretched on tenters to dry them and make them the right size and shape.

Most of the finished blankets were transported to London in heavy wagons, which then returned loaded with wool from the fellmongers in the capital. There was a good export market for Witney products. Arthur Young, the industrial and agricultural expert, writing in 1768, said that the best and most expensive blankets went to Spain and Portugal. Cheaper lines, which were still highly serviceable and attractive, were 'duffle stripe' and 'point' blankets. These were popular with the North American Indians, and Hudson's Bay Company placed regular orders with Witney weavers. The Indians were particularly fond of the duffles, which were sent out in pairs joined together, but with a hole in the middle of the join, so that they could be slipped over the head and worn as a warm cape. The weavers knew that the Indians liked the richly-coloured, broad stripes, and tried various combinations of dyes. By the 20th century the tradition had evolved of using indigo, yellow, red and green bars at each end of the white blanket. Less exotic Witney products were covers for wagons and barges, horse-blankets and water-repellent capes; all these were made of heavy cloth, which had not had all the grease removed, and therefore kept the rain off. Another successful Witney enterprise was mop-making.

The growth of the woollen industry was clearly reinforced by the fast-flowing river Windrush, which could provide water power for fulling mills on its banks between Witney and Burford. Alfred Plummer, in *The Witney Blanket Industry*, 1934, suggests that broadcloth weaving flourished here because there was no guild of weavers in the town, so that, apart from the general laws concerning weights and measures, very little in the way of restrictive practices existed. This allowed the industry to grow and competition to flourish. It is even possible that weavers from the older, but more restricted centres like Coventry may have moved to Witney in order to practise their trade unhampered by the rule of guilds.

This may have been a happy state of affairs in many ways, but during the 17th century the weavers found they had to contend with considerable fraud and malpractice. The Trade Commissioners, reporting in 1640 on the state of 'the clothing industry in England', found that frauds in the manufacture and dressing of cloth were causing a decay in the industry. Although alnagers (special inspectors) existed to insure that cloth was of a proper standard, they sometimes collected their

fees without carrying out their inspections, and were often dishonest enough to accept bribes to pass inferior cloth. In 1641 the blanket weavers of Witney petitioned the House of Lords about a patent for the sealing of their blankets, saying that 'Wm. Howes, now deceased, and his son' had been enriching themselves by raising the price for inspecting and sealing each bundle of blankets from 2d to 6d, and had also made money out of 'fines and exactions'. Their Lordships ordered 'that the patentees shall forbeare to lay any imposition upon the said Blankets made or to be made in that Toune until the pleasure of this House be further known'.

The Commissioners of Trade decided that the state of the industry would be improved if corporations were granted to sixty towns, including Witney, with paid officers to regularise standards. Nothing came of this idea, at least in Witney, and in 1670 the town's blanketers again petitioned for improvements, this time to the Earl of Clarendon, then Chancellor of England. They complained about 'the low condition of this poore towne which hath heretofore bin a place of great trading and hath yeelded much reliefe not only to the poore Inhabitants, but to the working poor about it'. They suggested that the river Windrush should be made navigable for boats as far as the Thames, that there should be improvements in the markets and fairs in the town, and 'that for the better and more orderly preservation of the Trade . . . in the keeping out of Forraigners and otherwise, there might be some settled government within the same by such way as your Lordship shall think most convenient.' What they really meant was that they wanted a closed shop, but their petition does not appear to have had any effect. Finally, in 1711, the blanket makers got their way, and Queen Anne granted them a Royal Charter of incorporation which formed the Company of Witney Blanket Weavers, to regulate the manufacture and sale of Witney blankets within twenty miles of Witney.

Though called a Company, the new organisation was not concerned with stocks and shares or joint production. Its members were independent individuals. Its job was to control such things as the size and weight of blankets, and the number of apprentices and journeymen a master weaver could employ. The Company held court and had the power to fine anyone breaking its by-laws, though sometimes the fines were remitted or reduced if the offender produced his money straight away. On 25 January 1737, for example, 'Elisha Whitlock was Returned for having twenty five Cutts in one stockful & was fined 20 shillings which he paid down but on his submission it was remitted to 6d.'

The Company maintained a warehouse in London, with a warehouse-keeper to organise storage of goods awaiting export or distribution.

In the 17th and early 18th centuries, blanket-making was in no way industrialised. Dr Robert Plot, the scientist and historian, writing in about 1677, suggests that in Witney there were threescore blanketers, who had at least 150 looms, 'employing 3000 poor people, from children of eight years old to decrepit old age . . .' Most of these would have been employed in the spinning of the wool rather than the weaving. Carding also kept a fair number of workers occupied. The small children probably worked at winding the yarn onto the bobbins. In 1788 the average number of looms per weaver was three, with eight being about the maximum.

The Blanket Hall, by W. Seely.

Alfred Plummer calculates that, when the Blanket Company was formed, there would have been about 180 looms working in and around Witney, directly employing 360 masters, journeymen and apprentices. Another two thousand or so men, women and children would have found work as carders, spinners, quill-winders and spoolers. There would also have been the fullers and tuckers who finished the cloth.

In the early years of the Blanket Company, meetings of its members were held in the Staple Hall Inn, but in 1720 they decided that they needed a headquarters of their own. They were able to purchase a house with a garden and orchard on the east side of the High Street for £85. The old house was pulled down and a grand new hall built in its place, consisting of 'the Hall', the 'Great Room' and the 'Assistance Room' with kitchens and out-buildings. The outside of the building was adorned with a one-handed clock, and on the roof was a wooden bell-turret with a cupola.

By the end of the 18th century mechanisation was creeping in. In 1782 the Company of Blanket Weavers purchased a horse-powered rowing machine for raising the nap on blankets, a job which had previously been done by hand, using teazles.

It was the great demand for cloth in the Napoleonic Wars that provided the biggest force for change: the overseas expeditions of Wellington's army must have caused a great need for blankets. When Arthur Young visited Witney in 1807 he remarked on the improvement of the industry, with the introduction of the spinning jennies and the spring loom 'by which one man does the work of two'. £4000 a year was earned by machinery, Young found, 'but in respect to the state of the working hands the medal must be reversed . . .' for mechanisation had not only cut down the number of workers employed, but pegged their wages to rates in force at the time of Young's previous visit, nearly 40 years before. Spinning was moving out of the cottages and into the mills, a disaster for the rural workers. John Early and Paul Harris were installing water-powered spinning machinery in New Mill around the 1790s. In 1818 a fire in New Mill caused severe damage, destroying £10,000 worth of valuable modern machinery.

The weaving process was not power-driven in Witney until about 1860. Power looms were only marginally faster than the spring or flying shuttle looms, which were, in fact, so efficient that they went on being used until well into the 1930s.

The advent of machinery effectively put an end to the authority of the Company of Blanket Weavers. Its rules and regulations just did not apply in the new industrial age. After a period of slow decline in attendance, the Hall was sold to Mr Edward Early for £200 in 1844, and the last few meetings took place back at the Staple Hall Inn, the Company's birthplace. The last recorded meeting was in October 1847.

From the 1660s the names of Collier, Marriott and Early dominated the Witney blanket industry. Enterprising and skilled master weavers from these families were important members of the Company, and eventually, with the arrival of mechanisation, became factory owners. Though rivals in a sense, they enjoyed a business relationship friendly enough to allow them to help each other out when the need arose, and to share big orders from Hudson's Bay Company, to the benefit of all. Socially, things were even better, for intermarriage often took place between the leading families, especially the Marriotts and the Earlys.

During the 1840s a new figure emerged onto the Witney woollen scene: William Smith (1815-1875), an orphan who was brought up by his grandfather, Henry Smith, a master tucker. William had some education at the dame school in Bridge Street, and then at the Blue Coat School till he was eight, when his grandfather's health deteriorated and he was sent out to work as a quill winder. A bright lad, he attracted the attention of Edward Early (1775-1835), who employed him as errand boy-spooler for four shillings a week. William was soon put in charge of all the weighing and inspecting of blankets for Edward Early. He writes: 'In the course of time my duties attended to the weighing in of wools, which taxed my arithmetic for a little time, the wools having to be weighed in packs, scores and pounds, and as my employer had now commenced a foreign trade in wools all of which were invoiced in hundredweights . . . At length the whole of the blanket department came into my hands for selection, classification, and packing, both for the home and foreign trade'. By the time he was 24 he was visiting the London blanket markets and learning about the more highly mechanised woollen industry of Yorkshire.

By the 1850s William Smith had acquired a small amount of capital as a result of a beer brewing business he was able to start in the almost disused Blanket Hall. When John George, who ran a small yarn manufacturing plant, became involved in debt, William was able to purchase his machinery. To this small donkey-powered machine he added an eight horse-power steam engine. This was the first use of steam power in the Witney woollen industry. Before then it had been thought too expensive to carry coal from the wharf at Eynsham to Witney. The speed at which businesses could be set up in those days is well illustrated by what William wrote about his first steam engine: 'I dug a well on the spot, erected a shaft, laid foundations for the engine, set the boiler on the flues, and had all complete for starting in 14 days.' Steam as a source of power proved a success. William was able to move to larger premises in Bridge Street and acquire bigger and more efficient steam engines.

The coming of the railway to Witney in 1861 reduced the price of coal and made steam power more economical.

By the beginning of the 20th century the blanket industry in Witney was run by the Earlys, the Marriotts and the Smiths. They were able to share contracts and help each other out with the spinning of yarn.

Over the years the name Witney came to be applied to a particular type of soft, good-quality blanket, and northern manufacturers did not hesitate to use it for their own products, even though they had absolutely no connection with the town. In 1908 the Witney manufacturers decided to try to keep the famous name for their own products. The Merchandise Marks Act of 1887 (an early trade description act) seemed to provide a good basis for a lawsuit against Rylands and Sons, the Manchester wholesalers, for selling blankets 'with a false trade description applied'. After a long legal struggle the Court came down on the side of the Witney manufacturers, and the northern companies had to give up using the name of Witney. Not all accepted defeat: the one way round the Court's decision was to set up premises in Witney, and this is what some of them did. The Witney Blanket Company set up the Butter Cross Works near the Church, to finish Yorkshire blankets to be marketed under the Witney label. Walkers, a Yorkshire firm, set up a mill in The Crofts, and Smith's Blankets went into partnership with Philips, another Yorkshire enterprise. Their association lasted until the 1970s, when the local industry contracted and they ceased trading.

In 1960 the firms of Early and Marriott decided to merge under the name of Charles Early & Marriott (Witney) Limited, continuing to make traditional blankets but also branching out into modern materials, methods and machinery. Now, in the 1990s, Earlys of Witney PLC are still in business: a remarkable example of a trade keeping family connections for over 300 years.

Convoy of blankets leaving Smith's Mill for the station. (OMS)

The Blanket Company Charter and Seal.
Photo Taunt

54

Collier's weaving mill, Corn Street, which later became part of a laundry, viewed from the playground of Batt School. (CG)

Charles William Early's mill on Wood Green, c1880. Drawn by W. Seely.

Commemorating 300 years of blanket weaving by the same family. (E)

Hand loom weaving in West End, 1890. One of these looms, now displayed at Cogges Farm Museum, is one of the oldest still in working order incorporating John Kay's 'flying shuttle'. Photo Taunt.

Power loom weaving shed, 1890. Taunt.

Fulling stocks. c1890. Taunt.

Lengths of blanket stretched to dry on tenters – 'on tenterhooks.' Taunt.

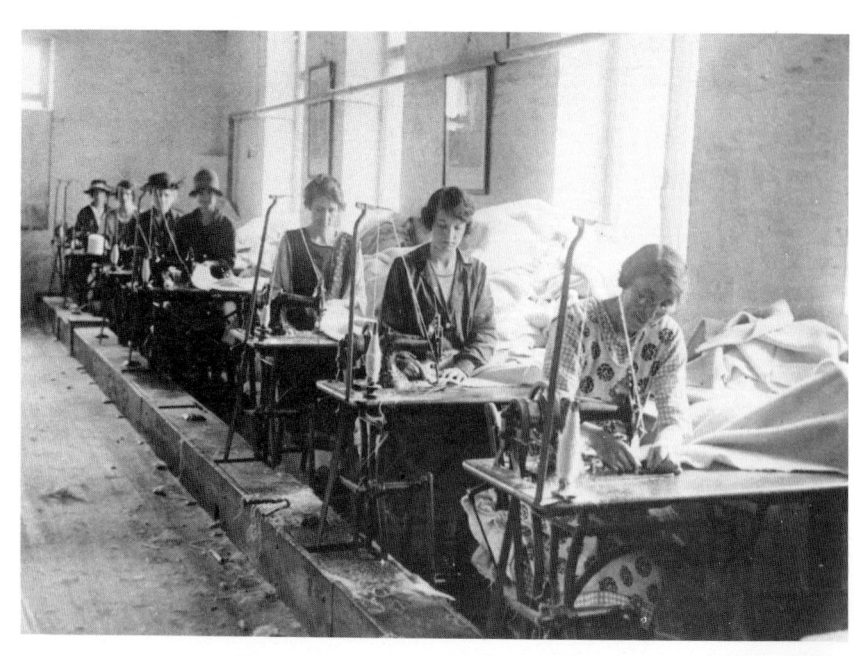

Whipping the ends of blankets, 1920s. (E)

The Witney Mill in Mill Street. (E)

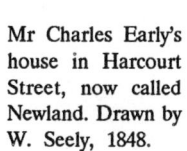

Mr Charles Early's house in Harcourt Street, now called Newland. Drawn by W. Seely, 1848.

Central detail of a portrait of Queen Anne by Sir Godfrey Kneller, presented to the Incorporated Company of Blanket Weavers by Simon, 1st Earl of Harcourt, High Steward of the Company, c1712. It used to hang in the Blanket Hall, and is now in the entrance hall of Early's. (CG)

Bridge Street Mill, founded by William Smith, now small industrial units. (CG)

Bridge Street Mill chimney. (CG)

The dray being loaded from the Newland warehouse, 1898. Drays continued to be used by the GWR to take goods to and from the station until 1950. Photo by Taunt. (OCL)

Richard Early, Master Weaver of Witney, 1964, beside a portrait of his great-grandfather, Charles Early. (BC)

The old Rectory, Church Green, built by the Rev. R Freind in 1723. Above the door is the crest of Jonathan Trelawney, Bishop of Winchester. Now part of Henry Box School. J. Buckler, 1825. (BL)

A South view of Witney Church, Oxfordshire.
Drawn & Engraved by John James Shury.

GOD'S HOUSE

It is probable that Saint Mary the Virgin, the Parish Church of Witney, was built by the Bishops of Winchester, and that work started some time between 1070 and 1100.

The original Church had a large nave without aisles. This nave of exceptional size is certainly of early Norman construction, though the small blocked-in window which can be seen from the north aisle, high up on the wall, is a single splayed window with a simple external rebate, and could be late Saxon. There may have been an earlier Saxon church on the site, but no evidence of this can be found in the existing masonry.

The north aisle and the porch were built in the late 12th century, and the Church was added to and extended throughout the next 200 years.

In the 13th century, at the time when Bishop Peter des Roches was laying out the new market place in Witney, the Church was largely rebuilt, with the addition of transepts and a central tower crowned with a graceful spire 156 feet high. As the town expanded during the same century, so the Church needed to be increased in size. A western aisle was added to the south transept, and later a south aisle was joined to the nave. It was about this time, also, that the chancel was rebuilt and enlarged.

The 14th century saw the addition of two chantry chapels. One was formed by extending the north transept, and the other was added to the north aisle, west of the porch.

The 15th century was a period of even more additions. An extra bay was built on to the south transept, and from it, on the eastern side, was added another large chapel parallel with the chancel. This chapel was removed in 1820, and the archway into it was walled up. Another 15th century innovation was a room built above the porch, with a fireplace in one corner; this was probably the living quarters of a chantry priest. Some time during this period a clerestory was added to the nave and transepts, which meant that the pitch of the roof had to be altered. All these alterations and additions to the Church are an indication of how prosperous the town of Witney was in medieval times.

Little in the way of embellishment to the building took place in the 16th, 17th or 18th centuries, though its fabric must have needed constant repairs. In about 1636 it was necessary to rebuild the spire, which had been 'taken off by a sudden storm'. The churchwardens appointed Humphrey Smith, a mason from Abingdon, to do the repairs, and agreed to pay him £200 to 'build up the spire of the said church to a substantial height and near its former glory'. The churchwardens, however, were not happy with his work, complaining that the repaired spire 'was not raised to its former altitude'. They refused to pay the full £200, keeping back £62. In support of Humphrey Smith, four witnesses - Richard Maud, James Partridge, Moses Brampton and William Edwards - certified to Bishop Bancroft of Oxford that the work on the spire was well worth £200, and that the reason it had not been restored to its former height was that 'the lower part of the steeple was falsely set by workmen appointed by the Bishop of Oxford'. Eventually, Smith was able to recover his money from 'the refractory spirits of Witney'.

Major restoration work was not again carried out in the Church until the 1860s, for during the first half of the 19th century the established Church of England was in a rather decadent state. Rectors were, more often than not, absentees. The long-suffering parishoners of Saint Mary's had to splash through deep puddles to get into their Church, and once inside they had to be prepared to share their pews with toads and spiders.

In Witney, at this time, the nonconformist churches played a more important part in the religious life of the community than the Church of England. The Congregationalists had built a new chapel in 1828, and 1850 saw the construction of the imposing new Wesleyan place of worship, which probably provided a strong incentive for the established Church to improve its own accommodation. In 1864 a new Rector arrived. His name was Francis Macaulay Cunningham, and he was a man of action who saw much that needed to be done in the parish. A radical restoration was set in motion, paid for by public subscription. George E. Street was appointed the architect, though it is doubtful if he ever came in person to supervise the work. The restyling of the chancel was taken from his design for Saint John the Baptist Church in Summertown, which was pulled down in 1924.

Several important alterations to Saint Mary's were made during the 1865 restoration. The large, five-lighted window at the east end of the chancel was removed, and replaced with a triple lancet window in the early English style. The chancel roof was altered: it had been low-pitched and lead-covered, matching the roofs of the nave and transept, but was converted into a steep-pitched roof covered in Stonesfield slates. W.J. Monk describes the restored chancel as being clothed in a dim religious light. In the nave, more light was let in by the unblocking of several partly blocked windows, and the removal of the gallery and organ that obscured the west window.

Over the centuries, countless burials had caused the level of the churchyard to rise several feet, so that the path to the north door had to be dug out as part of the restoration work. Francis Macaulay Cunningham wrote on October 24 1867: ' . . . had an army of men at work, lowering the paths both from the entrance gate to the north door and from our steps [the old Rectory steps] to the west door. We lowered the churchyard all round some two or more feet.'

Some of these restorations might be regarded as vandalism by 20th century opinion, but at least the parish was left with a dry, light and airy place of worship.

While Saint Mary's was going through its phase of neglect and dilapidation, the people of Wood Green acquired a brand new church on their doorstep. Holy Trinity was built in 1849, as a result of the efforts of the Rector, Charles Jerram, who felt that Saint Mary's was rather a long way for Wood Green residents to walk. In 1864 Bishop Wilberforce conducted a Confirmation service at Holy Trinity instead of Saint Mary's, because of the deplorable state of the latter. This event coincided with the arrival of Francis Macaulay Cunningham, and no doubt spurred him on in his determination to set the Parish Church to rights.

St. Mary's Church seen from the River Windrush. Drawn by W. Seely in 1851 from an old engraving.

LEFT: Monument to William Blake of Cogges and his family. BELOW: Small stone (now out of place), marking the grave of Robert Yates, Gentleman, who left goods and chattels worth £537 18s 4d in his will. (Both CG)

The carillon, like a giant musical box, still plays hymn tunes every three hours. (CG)

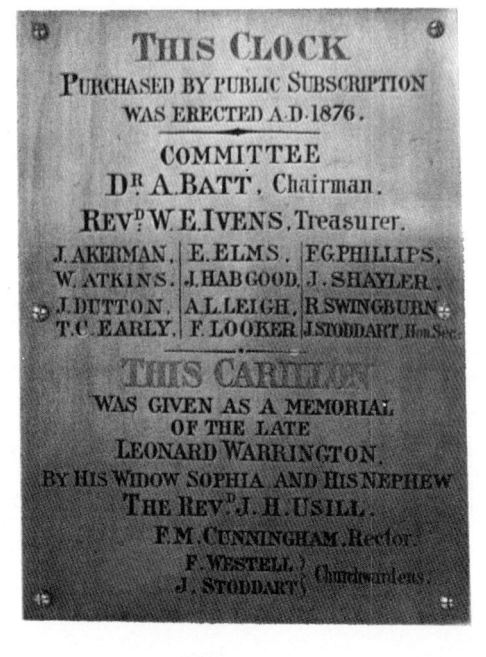

Holy Trinity Church, Wood Green, built 1849. (JG)

Holy Trinity Church from the Woodstock Road. (JG)

Site of the Friends' Meeting house, Wood Green. Now a private dwelling. (CG)

Gravestones in Friends' burial ground. (CG)

THE DISSENTERS

As far back as 1521 we can see signs of the important part played by nonconformist churches in the religious life of Witney. In that year, certain townspeople were accused of reading heretical literature. William Gune and his wife, along with John Baker, were accused of reading a treatise upon the Paternoster, and on another occasion John Baker was charged with reading the Epistle of Saint Peter in English. Another Witney man denounced for his heretical ideas was John Brabant, who may well have been a Flemish weaver who settled in England to escape the religious persecution of his own country.

There were many Quaker families in the district by the latter half of the 17th century. They held their meetings at the house of Kester Hart, which oral tradition places in Meeting House Lane, now called Marlborough Lane. There is no documentary evidence for this, and it seems more probable that the first meeting house was in a group of buildings called 'Old Housing' in Wood Green. The records of the Society of Friends show that John Hart, son of Kester Hart, transferred property in 1677 to Thomas Minchin of Burford, John Harris and Silas Norton, and also that Thomas Minchin gave £383 towards this newly-established meeting house. At the same time the parish records of Saint Mary the Virgin show entries with the words 'Buried among the Quakers in Hailey'. Wood Green was, at that time, within the parish of Hailey. During the 18th century all protestant places of worship tended to be called meeting houses, so the name Meeting House Lane does not in any way prove that the meeting house was a Quaker one. The Wood Green building was the home of the Witney Quakers until 1966, when, sadly dilapidated, it was sold to developers. The little graveyard remains, however, and still belongs to the Society of Friends. John Hart was one of the Quakers who sailed with William Penn, to found the new settlement of Pennsylvania.

The 'meeting house' in Meeting House Lane certainly existed, and is now used as a Scout hall. By 1712 it was used by the Independents or Congregationalists under the leadership of Rev Samuel Mather.

Another centre of nonconformity for the people of Witney was Cogges. The living of that parish fell vacant in February 1668, due to the death of the Vicar, John Parkinson. At the time the manor of Cogges was owned by Francis Blake and his son William. Their steward, Richard Crutchfield, took the opportunity of inviting some nonconformist ministers to preach in the Church. This led to what might be called an almighty row later in 1668. Thomas Gregory and his brother, Dr Francis Gregory, Master of the Grammar School, encountered Richard Crutchfield in the Church, and a heated verbal exchange took place, which ended with Crutchfield declaring that the clergy of England were none of Christ's ministers, and leading the greater part of the congregation out of the building. 'Come,' he said, 'the word of God is as good in a house as in a church.' From then on, Anabaptist services were held once, and sometimes twice a day, in the Blakes' manor house.

It would appear that neither Francis Blake, who died in 1693, nor his son William remained nonconformists, for in their wills, in which they left numerous benefactions to the people of Witney and Cogges, there is a provision for a supplement to the income of the incumbent of Cogges, on condition that he catechised the children of the parish regularly. In 1682, when Bishop Fell inquired into the state of nonconformity in Cogges, only two Quakers and one Anabaptist were listed.

The early years of the 18th century were boom years for dissent. The Congregationalists built their first chapel in 1715, with 'congregations estimated as between 400 and 500, and of these 30 are said to be gentlemen, ye rest tradesmen, farmers and labourers'.

There was something of a decline in support for the nonconformist churches during the next few decades, for when in 1738, Robert Freind DD, Rector of Witney, replied to a questionnaire sent out by Bishop Secker of Oxford, he reported that there were 40 families of Presbyterians, Independents and Anabaptists, all generally going to the same meeting house in the town of Witney. 'Two of the most zealous families which supported the Presbyterian interest there are extinct,' he commented, 'and so are some of lesser note among the dissenters, but none of late years have left the church, so their numbers must decrease. Most of 'em come occasionally to church, especially at sermon time. I have once among the rest seen their teacher there. There are also 30 Quaker families.'

In spite of Robert Freind's predictions, nonconformity in Witney did not die out. Far from it: there was to be an enormous resurgence at the end of the 18th century, inspired by the preaching of the great religious reformer, John Wesley. He had been curate at South Leigh in 1725, and knew the area well. Between 1764 and 1789 he preached in Witney regularly almost every year, sometimes indoors and sometimes in the open, and had a particular affection and respect for his numerous followers in the town.

How much of the rise of Methodism can be attributed to the great storms of July 1783 is hard to say. The facts are certainly uncanny. On 29 June 1783, Richard Rodda, one of Wesley's travelling preachers, was addressing a congregation at Wood Green, and felt impelled to say 'My dear friends, take notice of what I am going to say: before this day month you will hear and see something very uncommon.' Less than a week later, on 2 July, there was a terrible thunderstorm. Two people were killed by lightning, and workers hay-making in fields near the town were struck senseless. There were further awe-inspiring thunderstorms on 10 and 11 July. John Wesley wrote in his diary: 'There were uncommon thunder and lightning here last Thursday, but nothing to that which were here on Friday night. About ten the storm was just over the town; and both the bursts of thunder and lightning, or rather the sheets of flame, were without intermission. Those who were asleep in the town were awakened, and many thought that the day of judgement was come. Men, women and children flocked out of their houses and kneeled down together in the streets.' Mr Rodda, whose prophetic words had made a tremendous impression, admitted 50 new members to the Society on his next visit, and John Wesley himself added 34. Those enrolling at this traumatic time were sometimes known as the 'Thunder and Lightning Methodists'.

The early Methodist meetings were held in a weaving shop, but by 1801 the congregation had outgrown this building, and a new chapel was erected in the High Street. This, in turn, became too small, and was replaced by the present chapel, which was designed by J. Wilson of Bath in Gothic style and inaugurated in 1850.

The old Wesleyan Chapel. The houses on either side have been demolished. Drawn by W. Seely.

The Roman Catholic religion has gained in importance in Witney during the 20th century. In 1915 No 1 Church Green was used as a meeting place for the monthly celebration of Mass by a visiting priest from Summertown. Later in the same decade Mass was held at the old Workhouse chapel, as there was a group of Portuguese Catholics in the town; they were engaged on building work at the new aerodrome.

In 1933 the Anglican school in West End was acquired and adapted to become Witney's first Catholic church. The parish priest of Eynsham conducted the services, for it was not until 1948 that Witney's own parish priest, Father John Roddy, was appointed. During his long term of service, plans were made to build a new church, and in 1975, four years after his retirement, the Roman Catholic Church of Our Lady and Saint Hugh was dedicated. Two ancient stones from Eynsham Abbey lie beneath the altar, as a symbol of the long association of the two parishes.

The Convent of the Sisters of Charity opened in Curbridge Road in 1959, closing in 1990. The sisters who lived there did pastoral work or taught in the Catholic primary school of Our Lady of Lourdes.

The present Wesleyan Chapel, built in 1850. The building on the left was the Post Office. Drawn by W. Seely.

Field House the Congregationalist Chapel, previously used by the Christian Scientists. From 1823-1857 this building was used as a private madhouse run by the Batt family. (CG)

The old Congregationalist Chapel, demolished in the 1950s to make way for a supermarket. (SJ)

Chapel in the burial ground, designed by William Wilkinson. (CG)

ABOVE: Primitive Methodist Chapel, Corn Street, about 1900. (TW) Part of the facade is still visible above the Swan Laundry shop. Worshippers can now go to the modern Chapel in Davenport Road.

LEFT: Congregational Chapel in Meeting House Lane. The old Chapel is now used as a scout hall. (CG)

BELOW: Our Lady and St Hugh's Roman Catholic Church, 1986. (CG)

The Welcome Evangelical Church in the High Street, 1986. (JG)

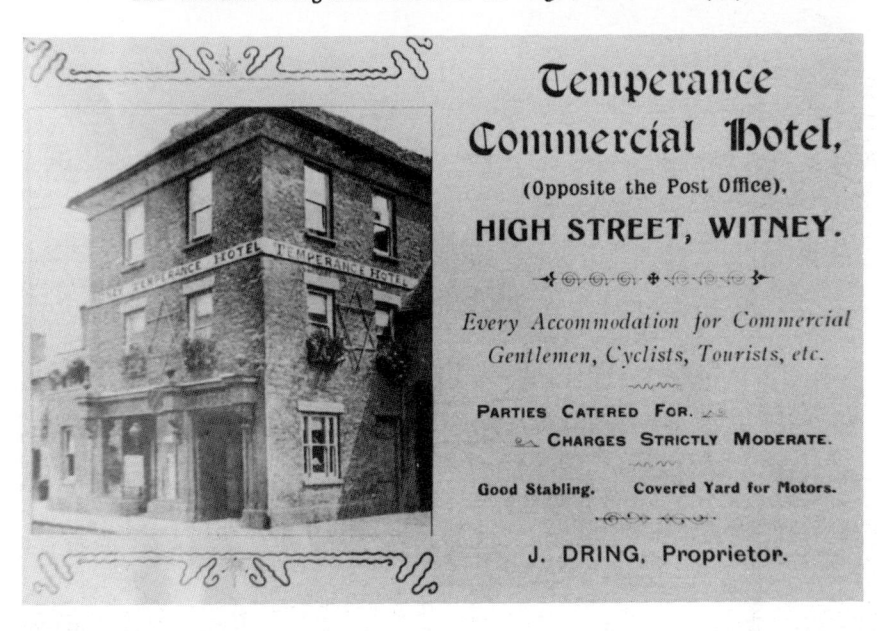

Temperance Commercial Hotel,

(Opposite the Post Office),

HIGH STREET, WITNEY.

Every Accommodation for Commercial Gentlemen, Cyclists, Tourists, etc.

PARTIES CATERED FOR.
CHARGES STRICTLY MODERATE.

Good Stabling.   Covered Yard for Motors.

J. DRING, Proprietor.

The Temperance Hotel (now Boots the Chemist), c1900. (OMS)

The station, starting point for the Witney Trips. (TW)

Witney Feast on Church Green c1900. It moved to The Leys soon after this date. (TW)

FUN AND GAMES

Present-day Witney has plenty of sporting facilities: a swimming pool, squash and tennis courts, bowling greens, football, rugby, hockey and cricket pitches. These amenities are mainly provided by the town and district councils. What forms of amusement were there for the townspeople in the past? When Giles wrote his *History of Witney* in 1852, he bemoaned the fact that 'the few remnants of our old sports and pastimes are rapidly disappearing', and went on to say that 'Witney has little to be recorded in the way of sports and pastimes'.

When the Bishops of Winchester came to stay in their Witney palace, it is probable that tournaments and jousts took place. There was hunting in Wychwood Forest for the comfortably-off, and poaching for the less law-abiding. Fairs and markets were a popular form of entertainment.

From the 13th century Witney had two fairs, one granted in 1202 and the other in 1231. According to the Hundred Rolls of 1279, these fairs took place on Ascension Day and on Saint Leonard's Day. These early fairs were for the serious business of buying and selling, and not for pure entertainment, like their present-day versions. Witney now has only one surviving fair, known as Witney Feast. This is a large funfair, and starts on the Monday after the first Sunday after 8 September. Traditionally, an open-air service is held to bless the fair on the Sunday before it opens, the clergy standing among the brightly-painted horses of the old-fashioned roundabout. The origin of Witney Feast really was a feast, for in 1243 Henry III gave two bucks for the Rector's feast at Witney. Nowadays, the Feast is held on The Leys, but earlier this century it took place on Church Green. Old Thomas Clarke, who was born in 1813 and was interviewed by the *Witney Gazette* in 1906, remembered it being held on Curbridge Down (on the left of the Burford Road). This move was probably during the 1860s, when the Down was also used for steeplechases.

Another fair that survived into the first decade of this century was the Mop Fair, a hiring fair where domestic and agricultural workers were engaged for the coming year. This tended to be an unofficial school holiday, and was held during the first week in October, on Church Green.

The coming of the railway brought about a new form of entertainment, the 'Witney Trip'. The first one was organised in 1876, by William Smith of Bridge Street Mills and Edward Smithman the stationmaster, when

186 people were taken by train to the seaside at Brighton. The Trips became an annual event, and continued until the outbreak of the First World War, paying visits to Weymouth, Bala, Weston-Super-Mare, Liverpool, Torquay, Blackpool, Southampton, Portsmouth and Hastings. There was an attempt to revive them in 1932, when 500 mill workers went to Brighton.

The forerunners of William Smith's Witney Trips were the outings arranged by the Rector, Rev F.M. Cunningham, to Nuneham in 1870 and '71. These excursions were for church workers, each one being entitled to bring a friend. Choir boys were eligible to go, but had to leave their friends at home. On the first outing the special train carried 95 trippers, and the next year 140 people went, leaving at 10.50am and arriving back in Witney at 10.30 in the evening.

The Leys, behind Saint Mary's Church, originally belonged to the Bishops of Winchester, and then passed to the Church Commissioners. In 1892 the Rector, Rev Foxley Norris, purchased the land for £1,000 as a place where the people of Witney could play 'manly games'. It was afterwards bought from a later incumbent as a war memorial after the First World War, and provided with facilities for cricket, football, bowls and tennis. There is now also a children's play area and paddling pool.

In the early half of the 19th century, before Holy Trinity Church was built, unofficial games of cricket, football and hockey were played on Wood Green - even on Sundays. William Smith, an otherwise exemplary young man, admitted to enjoying these guilty pleasures, explaining in his autobiography that 'there was ample space for any game selected, the only peace authority at the time was a Beadle, "John Beachey", whose visits to Wood Green were few and far between.'

Edward Smithman, the stationmaster from 1869 till his sudden death in 1886, was not only one of the founders of the Witney Trip, but also a great organiser of cultural events. He was secretary of the Natural History Society, he started the Witney Chess Club, and he was a prime mover in setting up a proper bathing place on the banks of the Windrush near New Mill. He also helped to raise money for a public library.

W.J. Monk mentions the annual battle that took place on 5 November between the Up-towns and the Down-towns, meaning those living south and north of the Windrush. No folk memory of this alarming-sounding event survives today. It seems to have died out around the beginning of the 19th century.

In that century drinking appears to have played a major part in Witney life, judging from the number of public houses. When the population of the town was about 4,000, there were some 30 public houses and inns. However, there were also active Temperance Societies, run by the Church of England and the Wesleyans, which offered alternative amusements to tippling, and alternative places for people to meet, including the Temperance Hotel and the Coffee Tavern. One particularly successful Temperance venture was a brass band, which was a popular attraction on important occasions, and featured smart military-style uniforms of blue cloth trimmed with gold.

At the turn of the century there were other bands too, attached to religious groups and factories, for brass band music was at the height of its popularity. Gradually they declined, until just the Town Band was left to carry on the tradition, enjoying its best years in the 1930s and 1940s. It is still in demand for local outdoor events, though players are now quite difficult to find.

The cinema or Kinematograph show had visited the town by 1898, and early this century Witney acquired its first cinema, the Electric Palace, at the Curbridge Road end of Corn Street. This first building was made of corrugated iron with matchboard sides and ceiling. There was accommodation for 800 people. The stage was 91 feet by 40 feet. The building had a gas engine dynamo and was all wired up for electric light.

A few years after its founding, the cinema moved to a more central position in Market Square, where it enjoyed many years of success as the Electric Theatre, then the Palace, before succumbing in 1985 to the pressures of television, video, high costs and dwindling audiences. However, in 1992 the Corn Exchange was equipped for cinema shows, which now take place regularly.

As for live entertainment, the old historians tell of religious plays and puppet shows held in or outside the Church in medieval times, though few details are known. Later, in the 17th century, plays were sometimes presented in local inns. One such performance ended in fearful tragedy. A group from Stanton Harcourt had drawn a good-sized audience to the White Hart, a Market Place inn which no longer exists. In the middle of the show, the floor collapsed under the weight of such a crowd, throwing large numbers down into the room below. Five people died and many were injured. This was in 1652, during the Commonwealth. John Rowe, Witney's Puritan 'lecturer', was quick to discover 'the hand of God' in the unfortunate playgoers' fate, and made great capital out of it in writing and in sermons.

During the Second World War there were large numbers of evacuee workers in the town, as well as troops on leave or stationed nearby. To cater for these lively young people, and to keep up morale on the home front, variety concerts and dances were arranged. There were boxing matches and other sporting events, including women's cricket. Occasionally, great musicians came down to give recitals.

At the beginning of the Second World War the London School of Dramatic Art was evacuated to Witney, taking up residence at 6 Church Green. Its principal, Miss Pickersgill, at once organised a professional repertory company and put on regular plays in a loft (with a strong floor) on the High Street. To find the theatre, the *Gazette* advised, 'go down the yard at the side of Messrs Tite's shop, and turn left past the budgerigars'. Though popular, the company ran into financial problems and had to close after a few years. Present-day live theatre is provided by the Witney Dramatic Society at the Corn Exchange, which was refurbished and opened as a public hall in the 1970s.

Witney Town Football Club proudly celebrated its centenary in 1985. Its traditional home was Marriotts Close, until it moved to a new ground on Downs Road in the early 1990s.

A game which has failed to survive in Witney is golf. A club was first formed in 1898, with a 9-hole course at Clement's Field. This proved unsuitable and, after being suspended for a time, the club was re-formed in 1906. The new 9-hole course, between the Woodstock Road and Cogges Wood, with natural hazards of hedges, ponds and trees, was laid out by the professional of the Oxford University Golf Club. The club house was a converted railway carriage. In 1907 there were about 70 members. How long the club lasted after that is not known; no trace of it remains apart from the iron head of a golf club which was ploughed up in the area.

The Bull and the Angel public houses, with Saltmarsh and Druce's delivery van outside the shop. The Bull Inn closed in 1969.
(TW)

The Three Horseshoes public house in Corn Street. The cottages on the left were pulled down to make room for Holloway Road.

The Black Horse Inn, West End. Drawn by W. Seely c1850.

The changing booths at the old bathing place on the banks of the Windrush. The indoor heated swimming pool was opened in 1973. (TW)

Witney Feast on Market Square, c1900, overflowing from Church Green, before it moved to The Leys. (OCL)

THE PALACE CINEMA

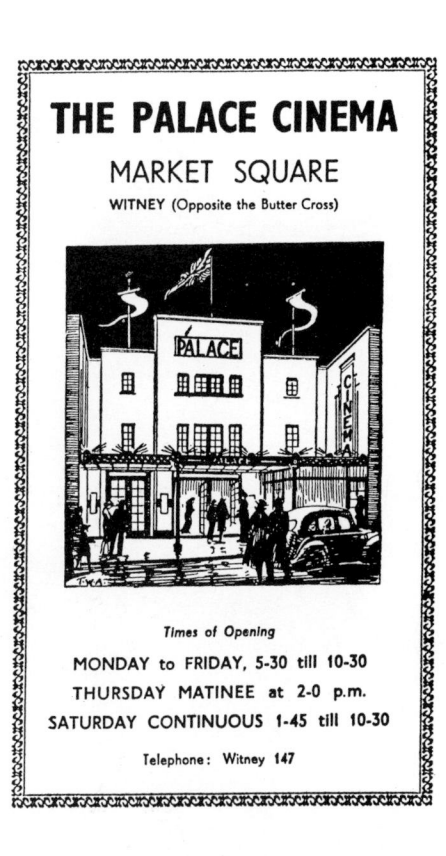

MARKET SQUARE

WITNEY (Opposite the Butter Cross)

Times of Opening

MONDAY to FRIDAY, 5-30 till 10-30

THURSDAY MATINEE at 2-0 p.m.

SATURDAY CONTINUOUS 1-45 till 10-30

Telephone: Witney 147

LEFT:
Advertisement for the Palace Cinema, Market Square, in its heyday.

BELOW:
The old cinema in Corn Street. (TW)

The old four-arched humpbacked bridge. (WTC)

The three-arched bridge replaced the old bridge in 1822; this was replaced in 1925 with a two-arched structure which was widened in 1967. (TW)

CROSSROADS

Much of Witney's significance stems from the fact that it lies on the main road from London to Gloucester and westwards, and is a crossing point of the river Windrush. The earliest roads tended to follow the tops of ridges on high ground, as lower-lying land was often marshy in wet weather, and the iron wheels of carts made a thoroughly unpleasant quagmire of road surfaces.

During the 16th century there was considerable trade in broadcloth woven in Witney and sold in the main London cloth market of Blackwell Hall. The carts or packhorses which transported the goods returned westwards with more wool for the weavers to process. The roads they travelled were nearly all in an atrocious state.

Each parish was responsible for the upkeep of whatever roads ran through it, and had to meet the cost out of the parish rate. Later acts allowed private companies to build roads and charge a toll, collected at gates or turnpikes.

The turnpike linking Witney and Oxford via Bladon was built in 1751; it is doubtful if it reached a high, or even an acceptable standard of engineering. Arthur Young described it thus: ' . . . repaired in some places with stones as large as could be brought from the quarry; and when broken, left so rough as to be calculated for dislocation rather than for exercise'. In 1779 he called the road from Witney to Northleach 'so bad that it is a scandal to the country'.

In spite of Arthur Young's adverse comments, turnpiking must have improved the roads, for traffic along them increased considerably. Fast stage coaches regularly passed through Witney on their way to Cheltenham and Gloucester. This caused some of the inns of the town to be enlarged to provide refreshment for passengers: the main coaching inns were the Crown, the Blue Boar, later to be renamed the Marlborough Arms, the King's Head, Staple Hall and the Court. By 1761 Thomas Costell was making use of the new turnpike road to Oxford by running a regular coach between Burford and London via Witney, using the causeway across the Thames at Eynsham. On this same causeway, in 1764, John Wesley's mare lost her footing and nearly gave her master a ducking. He was riding from High Wycombe at the time, on his way to preach in Witney. Five years later the crossing became a routine instead of a hazard, for the Swinford toll bridge had been built, and Mr Timson of Burford was running a regular stage wagon across it.

By the beginning of the 19th century things had greatly improved, and a series of good turnpike roads radiated from Witney. Each road had its own toll house or 'pike house', as they were known locally. One was at the foot of the hill leading to Wood Green, and belonged to the Burford-Campsfield Road Trust. Another, controlled by the Charlbury Roads Trust, was in West End. A third pike house was situated on the corner of Oxford Hill and Church Lane in Newland. This gate served to extract tolls on the Newland-Botley road. Toll prices were set by Act of Parliament. In 1812, when the Newland-Botley road was realigned to avoid Wytham Hill, the toll charges were: carriages with four wheels fourpence; carriages with two wheels twopence; horse, gelding, mare, ass one penny; ox, bull, cow, steer, heifer a halfpenny and calf, swine, sheep, lamb a farthing.

With growing competition from the railways, toll roads became less profitable, and a Parliamentary commission made recommendations that roads should be 'deturnpiked', though it was not until 1880 that the Newland-Botley road was freed of its tolls and the pike house was sold for £50. It was pulled down in 1947 when the road was widened.

Twentieth century travellers to Oxford can now use the A40, opened in 1947, which by-passes Eynsham to enter the City by the northern route. Heavy traffic in the centre of Witney became more and more of a problem as A40 users poured through in cars and lorries on their way between the west and London. This situation was much improved by the opening of Witney's own bypass at Easter 1977.

The canal age had its effect on Witney, though the proposed canalisation of the river Windrush to link the town to the Thames never took place. A small spur canal from the Thames to a wharf at Cassington meant that Witney was only six miles from a waterway system which extended to Birmingham by way of the Oxford and Grand Union canals, and opened the way to the industrial wealth of the Midlands and its coalfields. By way of the Thames, the great markets of London and the world became much more accessible. In 1824 the Oxford canal authorities gave the coal merchants of Witney a premium of four shillings a ton, to stave off competition from the Thames and Severn canal's wharf at Lechlade.

The canals' monopoly on cheap transport was short-lived, for in 1861 the railway came to Witney. It only came after much wrangling between the Great Western Railway and the London and North Western Railway. As early as 1836 a line connecting Tring, Oxford, Witney and Cheltenham was proposed, but nothing happened, on account of rivalry between the different companies. By the 1850s matters had become urgent: it was essential for Witney to be linked to the outside world by railway, if the local blanket industry was to remain competitive with its Yorkshire rivals. Not only would the transport of the finished products be cheaper, but the cost of bringing coal to the town would be much reduced. Without cheap coal, there could be no real modernisation of the woollen industry, to take advantage of steam power.

After a public meeting held in Witney in December 1858, the Witney Railway Company was formed under the chairmanship of Walter Strickland of Cokethorpe Park. Most of the capital for the new company came from local businesses: blanket makers, brewers and bankers all played their part.

The new line, opened in November 1861, was just over eight miles long, and ran from Yarnton, where it joined the Oxford, Worcester and Wolverhampton Railway, to a station in Witney near the Church and just below Mount House. In 1873 the line was extended to Fairford in Gloucestershire. At this time a new station was built to the south of the Church, and the original station became a goods yard.

For people living in the villages surrounding Witney, the railway was of little help in getting to the town's weekly market. They were catered for by regular horse-drawn carrier services, which left the various public houses in Market Square, following set routes to the villages. Later, of course, motor buses took their place.

The railway was a success, providing passenger services as well as the much-needed goods trains, and taking on a particularly important role in wartime. It ceased to be a Witney enterprise in 1890 when the Company sold the line to the GWR, which already provided the rolling stock. It survived nationalisation after the Second World War, but not for long. Better roads and the spread of car ownership led to a decline in business. British Rail policy dictated that passenger services should close down in 1962, and goods trains were finally stopped in 1970. The rails were removed and the 1873 station bulldozed; a few buildings still remain in the old goods yard, to remind Witney people that their town once had a railway.

Milestone near Staple Hall on the turnpike road to Camphill. (CG)

Newland before the widening in 1947. (TW)

The pike house on the corner of Church Lane (centre right), which was pulled down in the 1947 road widening. (OCL)

Staple Hall, originally a coaching inn. (CG)

Stables at the back of what was the Crown Hotel. The whole block was demolished in 1980 to make way for Langdale Gate. (OM)

LIST OF CARRIERS.

NAME OF CARRIER.		START FROM.	DAYS & TIMES.
Alvescot	Farmer	The Tea Mart	Thursday 5.
Asthalleigh	Mills	Coffee Tavern	Thursday 4.
Aston	Sparrowhawk	Bull	Thursday 4.
Bampton	Bryant	Holly Bush	Thursday 5.
Bladon	Nappin	Cross Keys	Thursday 3-30.
Bradwell	Farmer	The Tea Mart	Thursday 5.
Bright Hampton	Douglas	Angel	Thursday 4.
Brize Norton	Wilkins	Coffee Tavern	Thursday 3-30.
Burford (Bus)	Paintin	Coffee Tavern	Daily 4-30
Charlbury	Hall	Coffee Tavern	Thursday 4.
Charlbury	Eeles	Coffee Tavern	Thursday 4.
Coate	Sparrowhawk	Bull	Thursday 4.
Coombe	Slatter	Marlborough	Thursday 3-30.
Curbridge	Bryant	Holly Bush	Thursday 5.
Ducklington	Douglas	Angel	Thursday 4, Friday 4.
Eynsham	Harris	Coffee Tavern	Thursday 3-30.
Faringdon	Boucher	Marlborough	Thursday 4.
Filkins	Farmer	The Tea Mart	Thursday 5.
Finstock	Hall	Coffee Tavern	Thursday 4.
Hailey	Hall	Coffee Tavern	Thursday 4.
Handborough	Nappin	Cross Keys	Thursday 3-30.
Hardwick	Burden	Bull	Thursday 4.
Kencott	Farmer	The Tea Mart	Thursday 5.
Langford	Farmer	The Tea Mart	Thursday 5.
Leafield	Pratley	Bull	Tues. 2, Thurs. 3, Sat. 3.
Lew	Bryant	Holly Bush	Thursday 5.
Milton	Pratley	Bull	Tues. 2, Thurs. 3, Sat. 3.
Minster	Pratley	Bull	Tues. 2, Thurs. 3, Sat. 3.
North Leigh	Townsend	Cross Keys	Thursday 4.
Northmoor	Douglas	Angel	Thursday 4, Friday 4.
Oxford	Buckle	Own House	Mon., Wed. and Sat. 9.
Ramsden	Millin	Holly Bush	Thursday 4.
Shipton	Pratley	Bull	Tues. 2, Thurs. 3, Sat. 3.
South Leigh	Harris	Bull	Thursday 3, Saturday 3
Standlake	Douglas	Angel	Thursday 4, Friday 4.
Stanton Harcourt	Burden	Bull	Thursday 4.
Stanton Harcourt	Batts	Cross Keys	Thursday 4.
Stonesfield	Townsend	Coffee Tavern	Thursday 4.
Woodstock	Putt	Coffee Tavern	Thursday 4.
Woodstock	Knibbs	Coffee Tavern	Thursday 4.
Yarnton	Putt	Cross Keys	Thursday 4.

THE TEA MART, MARKET PLACE, WITNEY.

The carriers formed an important link between Witney and the outlying villages. On Thursdays the public houses near the market stayed open all afternoon, so passengers could have a drink while waiting for the carrier's cart.

WITNEY AT WAR

Witney has been a peaceful place for most of its existence; just occasionally it has been caught up in some national drama, though never in a starring role.

The Norman Conquest had little effect on the people living on the estate of the Bishops of Winchester. As the Bishops had Norman connections and sympathies even before the Conquest, they did not have to relinquish their estates to Norman lords as many Saxon thegns did, and so no drastic changes took place.

By the middle of the 12th century England was in a state of civil war as Stephen and Matilda fought over the throne. Henry of Blois, Stephen's brother, was Bishop of Winchester at the time. When Stephen refused to appoint him as Archbishop of Canterbury, Henry deserted the King and sided with the Empress Matilda.

It was an age when the art of war consisted of laying siege to castles. Henry of Blois turned his large manor house in Witney into something resembling a castle. The sight of the great new fortifications to the Bishop's Palace must have caused much apprehension among Witney people, as well as speculation as to who the rightful claimant to the throne really was. However, the rather uneventful conflict was fought out on other ground than Witney's.

In 1551, Witney was one of the stopping-places for Lord Gray of Wilton, as he led 1,300 troops down to Devon to deal with Prayer Book rebels. He summoned all the country gentry to Witney for a meeting, presumably to warn them to be on the lookout for popish influences. The event must have caused quite a stir in the town.

In the late 16th century attempts were made to get the peace-loving people of Witney to rise up against the landowners who were enclosing the open fields for sheep-runs. Caswell had been enclosed by the Wenman family, and large parts of Hailey had also been enclosed. In 1596 Barth Steere of Hampton Gay tried to organise an uprising by the poor to tear down the enclosures. In his zeal he told his supporters that there were 100 men of Witney who would 'go with them to throw down enclosure'. His brother John, who lived in Witney, did not agree with him. In the event John was right, for the Witney men failed to put in an appearance. John Harcourt (gent) of Cogges, who was later accused of offering to be their leader, denied all knowledge of the plot. The uprising fizzled out.

Anger against further enclosures was more forcefully expressed in March 1761, when a mob gathered at Northleigh Heath and threatened to pull down the enclosure fences. The troops were called in, the Riot Act was read, but still the mob stayed on to shout insults at the officers and soldiers. After an hour the Justices ordered the soldiers to disperse the mob and to take the ringleaders. Nine of them were arrested, and the whole affair ended without serious bloodshed.

There was one other occasion when the population of Witney got angry. This happened in 1800, when the price of grain was the cause. After remaining fairly static throughout the 18th century, it rose to unheard-of heights during the last decade. In Witney, a peck of flour cost 2s 0d in 1787. The price in 1798 was 2s 7d, and by 1800 it had gone up to 4s 6d. This rise in price was the result of a series of disastrous harvests. It is not surprising that people were incensed. Who better to take their frustration out on than the miller? A gang from Witney marched to the mill at Fawler and threatened the miller there.

Witney escaped fairly lightly during the Civil War, for no great battles were fought here. However, when King Charles I was based at Oxford, he was in constant need of food and equipment for his troops, and this placed a severe strain on the resources of towns in the area. From the Royal Ordnance Papers it is possible to get some idea of the demands made by the Royalist army. Witney was expected to provide it with planks and timber, and to surrender the weapons belonging to the town's trained band. These bands had been set up by law all over the country, and equipped by the towns to be used in case of riot or other national emergencies. The Royal Ordnance Papers contain an inventory of the arms taken from each town; the Witney list reads like this:

Powder	*1 barrel*	*Brests*	*6*
Match	*10 skeynes*	*Backs*	*5*
Musket shot	*1 barrel*	*Head peeces*	*6*
Muskets	*36*	*Sords*	*6*
Bandeleers	*23*	*Long pikes*	*17*
Bird peece	*1*	*Clubb staffe*	*1*
Carbines	*2*	*Broken sord*	*1*
		Girdles for Bandeleers	*4*

8 Dec 1643.

In the register of burials there are references to soldiers being buried in Witney: two in April 1643 and three in October of that year.

During June 1644 there was much to-ing and fro-ing around Witney, as the King tried to escape from Oxford, though the main troop movements passed north of the town on their way from Woodstock to Burford. While in Burford, the King billeted himself for the night at the house of William Lenthall, the Speaker of Parliament, who later, during the Commonwealth, leased the manor of Witney. King Charles then marched on to Bourton on the Water, but found the way north blocked by General Waller's troops. He decided to return to Oxford, and on the nights of 18, 19 and 20 June he stayed at the White Hart, Witney. At the time the Royalist army comprised 6,000 men, and they were reinforced with a further 4,000 during the King's stay in Witney. On 19 July the peace of the town was again shattered, this time by Waller's troops, who camped there overnight.

Cromwell himself may well have passed through Witney in May 1649, on his way back to Oxford after suppressing the Levellers' revolt at Burford. There was a strong nonconformist element in the town at the time, represented by many of the leading families, such as the Gunnes and the Warrings, who would have been on the side of the Parliamentary army. But there is no record that the people of Witney ever took an active part in the turmoil of the Civil War. They probably hated whichever army was in the district.

In the 1860s fear of war led to military preparations all over the country. Witney's contribution was to form a volunteer Rifle Corps. Called the 5th Oxfordshire, it took part in camps, exercises and parades for several years.

The impact of the great 1914-18 conflict must have been the same on Witney as on most other small towns, with enormous patriotic jubilation giving way to realisation of the futility and waste of war. Young men volunteered to go to the front. A committee for Belgian refugees was set up, and the refugees themselves were housed at No 64 Bridge Street.

No 31 West End was a public house called the King of Prussia. The name obviously had to go, so it was called the Czar of Russia instead. Later still another change became necessary. and it acquired the patriotic (and inoffensive) name of House of Windsor.

It seems that there were some evacuees from London in Witney in the latter part of the war. In October 1917 the school inspector visited the National School on Church Green and found 'the offices' (presumably the lavatories) in a dirty condition: the seats needed scrubbing and the ledges needed dusting. Mr Hayter, the head teacher, explained that the trouble was caused by London children, who had come to escape the air-raids and were 'not under the usual control'.

An important event late in the war was the building of Witney Airfield, on the land now taken up by the Smith's Industries complex north of the town. German prisoners of war were brought in to level the site, and the buildings and hangars were put up by Portuguese workers. The airfield became operational as a Training Depot Station for the Royal Flying Corps aircrew in March 1918. From then on Witney people became accustomed to the sight and sound of Bristol Fighters, Sopwith Pups and other aircraft, and to meeting the young trainee pilots in the local shops and public houses.

The Belgian refugees, German prisoners and Portuguese workers were not the only foreigners to be seen in and around Witney in those days for, in April 1918, according to the Witney Gazette, there were Americans and Canadians stationed at the airfield. Social life in the town was much improved, and baseball matches were played on The Leys.

However, the grim reality was that 157 men from Witney lost their lives. They are commemorated on the War Memorial on Church Green.

September 1939 found Witney quietly preparing for whatever unpleasantness was to come. As in every other town, its residents had to get used to blacking out their windows every night, digging for victory and economising on food and fuel, as rationing became more and more severe.

Dedication ceremony, Witney War Memorial. (TW)

The armed forces claimed large numbers of young men, who soon found themselves in parts of the world they had barely heard of and certainly had not expected to visit. Thirty five of them lost their lives, some in the Far East, two in North Africa and some in Europe, including six who died in Normandy during the fighting that followed the D-Day landings in the summer of 1944. Men and women from Witney served in many different branches of the Forces.

At home, Air Raid Precautions had to be organised. Wood Green housed the headquarters of No 4 Area ARP Civil Defence Services of Oxfordshire. A large concrete air raid shelter struck a discordant but necessary note on Church Green. The unmusical tones of the siren were heard on the first Monday of every month at 1pm sharp, when testing took place.

In November 1940 ARP members were called upon to test their skill, for a lone enemy aircraft made a surprise raid on the town centre. A large number of houses were damaged, and windows were shattered in the Church, the Council Offices, the Police Station and the Grammar School, as well as in a number of shops. Fortunately no-one suffered serious injury, though some cuts and bruises were reported.

Luckily for Witney, this was the only time bombs fell in the town. In fact, it was considered to be a safe area, and large numbers of evacuees arrived from London within days of the outbreak of war. At the end of September 1939 there were 400 in the area: 200 unaccompanied school children and 200 others, mostly mothers with young children. An Evacuation Relief Fund was opened; it was much needed. That first Christmas of the war two huge parties for children were held, one at the Corn Exchange and one at the Drill Hall (now the Langdale Hall). About 850 young guests met Father Christmas, yelled at Punch and Judy, and gazed at the beautifully decorated tree.

In September 1940 the boys of Ashford Grammar School, Kent, arrived. After spending their first night sleeping in the Palace Cinema, they were taken to their billets, and later to Witney Grammar School (now Henry Box), where a two-shift system enabled the two schools to share buildings and sports facilities for several months.

Witney people were quick to support the war effort in every way. The Women's Voluntary Service worked hard to collect money, bandages and clothes for the Witney Red Cross Hospital Supply Depot, to send wherever they were needed. Women's Institute members knitted with a will.

Men aged up to 65 were invited to join the Local Defence Volunteers, later to be re-named the Home Guard. Many responded, and found themselves taking part in regular parades and exercises, as well as doing more mundane jobs, like filling sandbags for Civil Defence purposes. On one exercise, reported in the *Oxford Mail*, they joined with the Civil Defence to repel simulated 'airborne troops'. 'Much of the fighting was in West End and Mill Street, and it was in Mill Street that some tear gas was used, to the discomfiture of some pedestrians and motorists'.

In 1940 an appeal for blood donors brought in 236 volunteers. Huge nation-wide fund-raising efforts were generously supported: among these were the Spitfire Fund, War Weapons Week and Warship Week. War Weapons Week in September 1941 featured parades of the Services, and Sounding the Retreat by the band of the Oxfordshire and Buckinghamshire Light Infantry. There were displays by the Town Band, the Brize Norton Band, the Home Guard and the ARP, as well as low flying and 'dive-bombing' over the town by the RAF. In addition, there were three dances, a variety concert, an exhibition, a military band concert, several cinema shows and a drumhead service on Church Green.

Witney Airfield played a vital part in the war effort, for it was used as a repair base for de Havilland aircraft. Tiger Moths, Hurricanes and Spitfires, among others, were brought in regularly for overhaul between 1941 and 1945.

A panorama of de Havilland's, 1943. (DD)

A strange spectacle in Market Square. This captured German aircraft was put on show in various towns for fund-raising purposes. (TW)

Leaving Witney station for the War, October 1914. (DD)

Troops on parade in Market Square, 1916. (TW)

Victory in Europe Day, 1945. (TW)

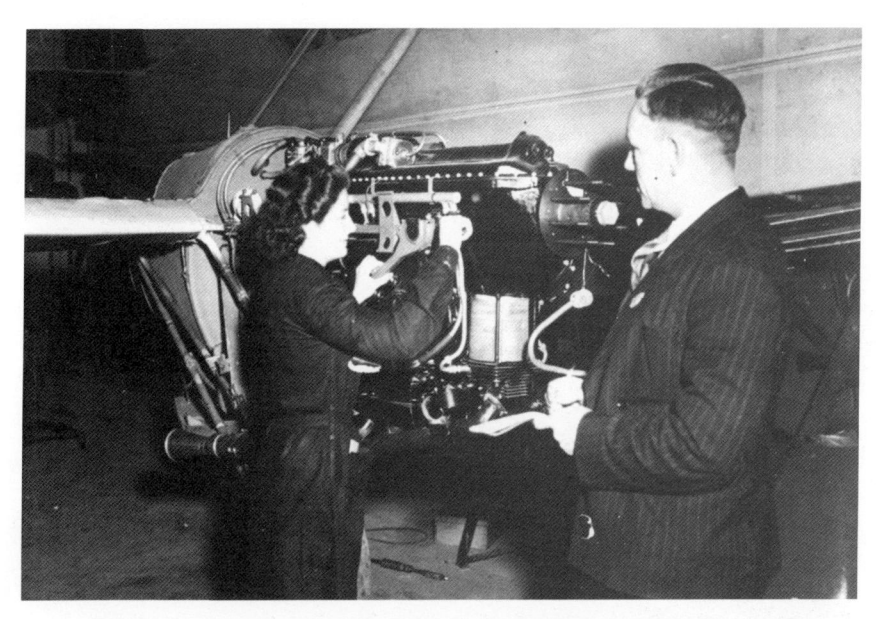

Work in progress at the de Havilland Works, Witney Airfield, 1943. (DD)

A wartime dance at de Havilland's; 'This photograph is censored — for record purposes only. Publication strictly prohibited' — in 1944. (DD)

The old Drill Hall has been thoroughly modernised and re-named the Langdale Hall. (CG)

A Second World War pill box stands guard over the Windrush, 1986. (JG)

OF COURT AND COUNCIL

In the first decade of the 13th century Bishop Peter des Roches formed the new Borough of Witney alongside the existing village.

In order to attract people to his new development he granted certain privileges to the inhabitants. The charter awarding these rights has not survived, but in 1256 another Bishop of Winchester, who was also a founder of towns, granted a charter to Newtown on the Isle of Wight, giving it the same liberties and free customs as those of Taunton, Witney, Alresford and Farnham. Under their charters the towns were allowed to have their own court with their own bailiffs, and to profit from the fines of the court, except for fines from the use of the pillory and the tumbril, which went to the Bishop.

The inhabitants of the Borough were also excused from having to attend the Bishop's manor court, which was compulsory for other residents of the manor, though they did have to attend the twice-yearly Bampton Hundred court.

The borough court became the form of local government during the middle ages, with its own officers. It was ruled by two bailiffs, who gave judgements and organised the affairs of the town, with the help of the other officers and the chief citizens of the Borough.

The rules made by the court were starkly down-to-earth. They were concerned with making people remove the dung-heaps outside their houses, and ensuring that any pigs running loose were ringed to prevent them from digging holes in the streets; all very necessary in an age when there was no inside sanitation, and not much outside either, except for an open drain which ran down the middle of the High Street and was crossed by many small footbridges.

The Tudor town was divided into five wards, each with a wardsman. Paternoster Ward consisted of the west side of Church Green and Market Place. East Ward was on the east side of the same streets, but included some of the High Street. West Ward was Corn Street and the west side of the High Street. The rest of the High Street formed Middle Ward. The Ward Beyond the Bridge went as far as Staple Hall and included the west side of West End.

The wardsmen were the equivalent of aldermen in larger towns. Their job was to report to the court minor offences, such as selling underweight loaves of bread or below-strength ale, allowing pigs to wander, causing minor breaches of the peace and blocking the road with dung-heaps. They were helped in their work by officials appointed by the court.

There were two ale-testers to check that the ale was fit for human consumption and not diluted. There were also two cardenars, whose job was to inspect all meat offered for sale.

Besides being responsible for keeping up standards in health matters and in weights and measures, the court was also in charge of maintaining standards in tanning and the manufacture of leather goods, and in the weaving of cloth. Officers were appointed to inspect cloth and leather, and deal with any unacceptable practices.

Under Tudor legislation the parish became the unit of local government, taking over from manorial rule. The Vestry became responsible for the administration of the Poor Law, and for the appointment of a parish constable and a surveyor of highways.

During the 16th century and the early part of the 17th, the borough court and the Vestry did not come into conflict as to who did which job, as they were, by and large, made up of the same people. With the growth of nonconformity in the town and the wane of the borough court in the mid-17th century, some conflict did arise between the two bodies, especially over the payment of poor relief. The Vestry insisted not only on its right to administer the funds, but on confining payments to Sundays after prayers. So those who failed to 'sign on' at Church were unable to collect their dole. The borough court retained control of the charities that had been left to it.

By the mid-17th century the borough court had gone into decline and, although it still existed until 1925, the function of local government was carried on by the Vestry, though the bailiffs administered some of the charities for the poor. The job of controlling the quality of cloth passed over to the Blanket Company. As in other small towns and villages, the Vestry struggled through the 17th and 18th centuries to administer the affairs of the town.

The borough court only had jurisdiction over the old Borough of Witney, which did not include Wood Green and the east side of West End. They were both in Hailey, and came under the jurisdiction of the manor court, as did the lower half of Corn Street, which was in the parish of Curbridge. It was not until the local government reorganisation of 1894 that the boundaries were changed to include Wood Green.

By the 19th century, drastic reform was needed in the organisation of local government to meet with the greater complexity of life. The Local Government Act of 1863 allowed for the setting up of Local Boards to take over the civic duties of the Vestry and oversee much of the new Victorian legislation. The Witney Board was replaced by the Urban District Council in 1895.

A large part of the work of the UDC concerned the provision of clean, safe drinking water for the townspeople. Until the beginning of the 20th century, all the drinking water in Witney came from wells. The problem was that they were all too often situated near the privies, and the pollution that resulted led to outbreaks of cholera. The wells belonging to the properties on the east side of the High Street were fairly free from contamination, as the burgage plots were long enough to allow a good distance between the wells and the privies. In Corn Street, however, conditions were more cramped, and the privies and middens tended to drain into the wells.

During the 1890s the Witney Board had an energetic sanitary inspector, Dr William Dyson Wood, who found that many of the town wells were in an unhealthy state. In the drought of 1894, numerous wells ran dry. Ninety houses in Corn Street had to get their water from a public well on Church Green, and of the 15 wells in The Crofts only two gave an adequate supply. In view of all these problems, the newly-formed UDC decided that a piped water supply was needed.

It was not until 1903 that the work was completed. A deep well was sunk near Apley Barn in the Windrush Valley. In order to provide the town with a greater water pressure, a grand brick water tower was built, with a large metal tank on the top, holding 80,000 gallons.

The new system opened with all due pomp and ceremony in late 1903, though the joys of this first supply were short-lived. Only a few months later, disaster struck. A poem from the *Witney Gazette* tells the sad story:

Water Tower,	Losing water,	Poor little lambs,
Tank on top,	Like a crock,	With names below,
Filled with water	To the council	So proudly raised,
Went off pop.	Quite a shock.	Dishonoured so.
Sudden strain,	Great sensation,	It's not our fault
Sides bent,	Council run,	Perhaps they'll say
Consequently	And people too,	But who will have
Big rent.	To see the fun.	To pay pay pay?

The 'names below' were those of the Urban District councillors on the plaque that was placed at the foot of the tower. It had cost the ratepayers £12, and had caused strong criticism to be voiced in the local paper.

The bulging Water Tower. (TW)

A second attempt to build a water tower had the same unfortunate result, but the third tower was a success, lasting until it became redundant with the opening of the Worsham waterworks, which solved Witney's water problems. The water tower was never able to supply enough water for the growing needs of the town, especially after the building of the Airfield towards the end of the First World War.

If water has been a source of concern, fire has always been a major worry in Witney. Even in Tudor times we find a hint of the problems in the court books: 'Order by the bailiffs that every householder in Witney to have standing or set without his street door on every night from this court day until 29 September next one tub, cowl, barrel, pail, pan or cauldron with water in readiness against fire on pain of 6d for every default to the contrary.' Whether this ruling about fire buckets was made in response to a particular fire, or just as a general safety measure, we shall never know.

The first serious fire in the town about which anything is known was in 1734. Monk says: ' . . . a calamity of rather a serious nature occurred at Witney. A fire broke out in a tallow chandler's shop, and before it could be subdued, 30 houses were completely destroyed.'

In 1875 the town at last got its own volunteer Fire Brigade: Herbert Smith, son of William Smith, the founder of Smith's Mills, was instrumental in forming it. He was well aware of the frequency of mill fires and, after a blaze in Bridge Street Mill, he and his colleagues decided that something must be done. Buckets of water were in no way adequate to deal with a house fire, let alone one in a mill. So they formed a group of volunteers, and obtained a fire engine. After that the townspeople had fewer worries about the risk of fire, though in 1879 the service was tested and found wanting. A fire broke out at the mop factory of T. and W. Early in the High Street, and destroyed it 'despite its being within a few yards of the river and behind the fire station in Millin's Yard. Two engines arrived too late, one having been delayed by the refusal of two individuals to lend horses to draw it.' The *Witney Gazette* does not identify the two unfriendly individuals.

The original Fire Brigade had its headquarters in Millin's Yard, behind what is now 101 High Street, and continued to operate from there as a horse-drawn unit until 1927. Its responsibility was for the municipal area of Witney only; in the 1920s this did not include Cogges or Newland. After a ruinous fire at Pritchard's Glove Works in Newland, which the Witney Fire Brigade refused to attend, the UDC stepped in to organise a larger Fire Brigade.

An old barn behind the Corn Exchange became the new headquarters, and a second-hand 1915 London fire engine was bought for £250. It lasted until 1937, when it was honorably retired in favour of a new engine which cost £900. The Fire Service now has a modern headquarters built for it in the 1960s on the Welch Way development.

The old Police Station, built 1860 by William Wilkinson, is now used by Henry Box School. The modern Police Station is in Welch Way. (CG)

The horse-drawn fire engine. (TW)

The old Fire Station behind the Corn Exchange. (TW)

Witney Mill after the fire of 1905. (TW)

The engine room at Pritchard's Glove Factory after the fire of 1926. Because Pritchard's was in Newland, which was then outside the boundaries of Witney, the Witney Fire Brigade could not attend. (TW)

The old wooden bridge across the Windrush on Langel Common, with Cogges Church in the background. In 1897 the bridge was replaced by an iron one. (TW)

The 1985 bridge. (CG)

Highworth Place. Early council housing built for ex-servicemen after the First World War. Originally the field was called Highworth Piece, and the rents from it went to support the poor of Highworth. (CG)

The Fire Station in Welch Way, built in the 1960s. (CG)

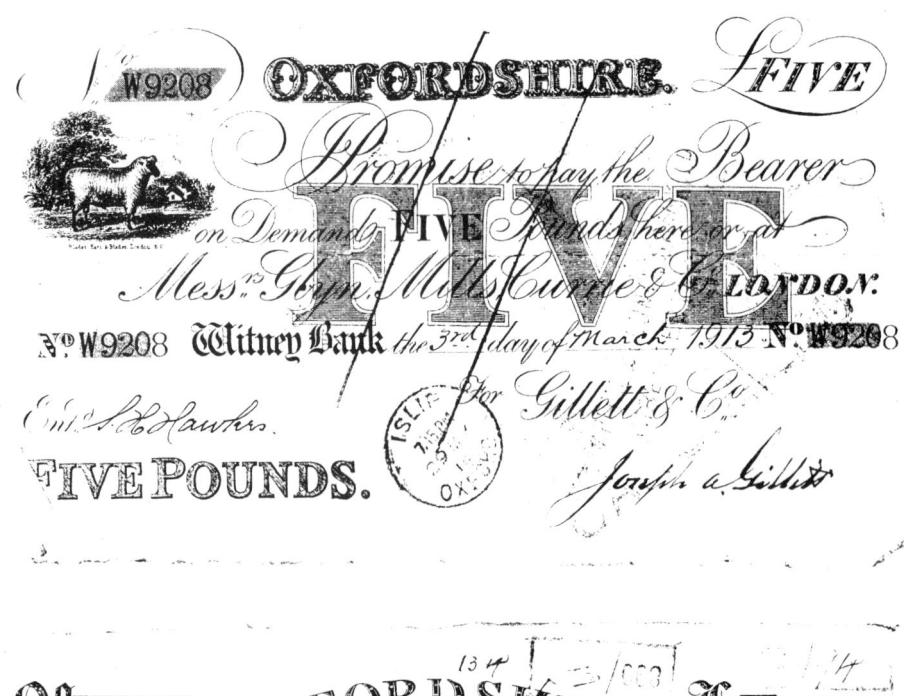

Five and ten pound notes issued by Gillett's Bank in Witney, 1913.
(OMS: Acc 951 & 949)

IN BUSINESS

Until modern times, Witney enjoyed its greatest prosperity in the Tudor period. During the latter half of the 16th century, while the country was regaining its strength after recurring bouts of plague, the town grew steadily.

Ever since the Black Death the Bishops of Winchester had farmed out more and more of their land to tenants, so acquiring income from rents rather than farm produce. By 1453 all the demesne had been let out. While the Bishops were actively engaged in agriculture, they kept meticulous account rolls, from which we learn that it was their practice to send unprocessed wool from their estates to markets in London and Winchester, though frequently large quantities were stored in Witney for years, before being taken away to be sold.

As the Bishops relinquished their agricultural role, so other entrepreneurs came forward to take their place. These new wool barons enclosed land for sheep, and were able to buy up wool from lesser farmers, who did not have the resources to send their product as far as the London market. The Bishops' lack of interest in wool production, combined with the inability of many small landowners and tenants to raise capital to market their wool in London, may well have been among factors encouraging the growth of Witney's weaving industry. If wool could be spun and woven in Witney and the finished cloth exported to the great City of London, then higher profits could be made from a cartload of woven cloth than from a cartload of unspun wool.

The 1530s and '40s were boom years in the cloth trade. Witney had one vastly rich man: Richard Wenman, 'a merchant of the staple'. In 1524 the total tax bill for the town was £55 3s 8d, of which a staggering £43 6s 8d was Wenman's contribution. When he died in 1543 he left over £2,000 in cash, as well as property in many of the surrounding parishes.

Although the Wenmans were by far the richest family in town, there were others who enjoyed great affluence in Tudor Witney. The Fermors were wool merchants with land in many neighbouring parishes. Thomas Fermor, who died in 1485, was buried with his wife in Witney but, although the family continued to hold land in the area throughout the Tudor period, they were not resident in the town.

After Wenman, the 1544 subsidy roll gives Edward Wilmot as the next richest resident: his coat of arms can be seen in the Church. He moved to Witney from Abingdon in about 1540. The Wilmot family had enclosed lands at Stadhampton and Chislehampton, and their money came from sheep and wool. Edward Wilmot was trading wool on the Calais market at the time of the fall of Calais.

By the middle of the 16th century the wealthy families tended to be cloth merchants rather than wool merchants: they included the Gunnes, Colliers, Pennys, Yates and many others. The occupations of 540 Witney residents during the period 1545-1609 are known: 46% of them were connected with the weaving industry.

Along with the prosperity of the clothiers the town grew in affluence and business flourished. Most trades were represented in 16th century Witney. There were bakers, butchers, fishmongers and haberdashers. Skilled building workers were to be found, as well as glovers, tanners, saddlers, smiths, cobblers and shoemakers. There was not much that a citizen from one of the surrounding villages could not buy in Witney. Many of the wealthy families had connections in London: one of these was the Box family, who later founded the Grammar School.

The 17th century did not get off to a good start, for in 1597 the parish register records 140 deaths, with the words, 'From the unknown disease that the Lord has inflicted on us. May He have mercy on us.' The average yearly number of burials for the end of the 16th century was 25, so 1597 was truly disastrous. Over the whole of the 17th century the total numbers of births and deaths in the town were about equal, with births exceeding deaths in some years and the reverse in others. During the 18th century there was a gradual improvement. The last year when more people died than were born was 1720; after that the birth rate rose steadily. There was an increase in prosperity over the whole country, and Witney was not left behind.

As the blanket industry grew stronger, so did trade. The most visible trace of this rising prosperity can be seen today in the fronts of the houses and shops in the older parts of the town, many of which date from the period between 1700 and 1840, though the backs of some buildings are considerably older. Georgian changes to frontages altered the roof line, to give more headroom to the upper storeys, so that many of these altered houses give the impression of being two and a half storeys high. These new house fronts tended to be given an ashlar or stucco finish, in an attempt to make them appear of more expensive cut stone. The wealthier merchants built themselves new houses at Wood Green and West End.

The 19th century saw the beginnings of many businesses, some of which are still flourishing in the town today. In 1796 the Witney and Oxfordshire Bank was established on the Hill. It later moved to the premises next to the Marlborough Hotel which are now occupied by Barclay's Bank. The founders of this first bank were the twin brothers Augustine William Batt (1774-1847) and Edward Batt (1774-1827), and John M. Buckshell. The latter probably ran the bank, while the Batt brothers put up the money. Unfortunately it ran into difficulties after a few years, and in 1815 the three principals were declared bankrupt. They were bought out by John Williams Clinch. The Clinch family probably settled in Witney around 1780, when John Clinch married a Witney girl, Hannah Ashfield, though their local connections may go back much further, as Oxfordshire parish registers record the name of Clinch from the early 17th century. The family were mostly engaged in farming. John Clinch is described as a banker in his will of 1827, but he was also a businessman dealing in wool, malting and farming, as well as owning public houses and land. He had two sons, James and John Williams. The latter became a banker after the collapse of Batt's Bank, while his brother James became a brewer.

The bank survived in the hands of the Clinch family until the deaths of John Williams in 1871 and his son (another James) in 1876. However, by 1867 it was in trouble, for John Williams had taken cash out of the banking business that was not rightfully his. When James died, his brother William found himself in a bad way financially, partly because the bank had been badly managed and partly because he had had to settle the gambling debts of one of his brothers. To solve his money problems he sold his controlling interest to Charles and Alfred Gillett, bankers in Banbury and Oxford. The bank then traded as Messrs Gillett and Clinch but, with the death of William Clinch in 1891, it became known as Gillett & Co.

Although the Gilletts' main bank was in Banbury, they were no strangers to Witney, for members of the family had farms at South Leigh. Theirs was not the only bank operating in Witney during the closing years of the 19th century. The Birmingham Banking Company established a branch in 1885, which became the Metropolitan Bank in 1894, and amalgamated with the Midland Bank in July 1914. Gillett's Bank was finally taken over by Barclays in 1903.

The Batt family settled in Witney in about 1735, and from then until 1903 there was always a member of the family practising medicine in the town. Dr Charles Dorrington Batt, (1845-1926), was the last of the line. Between 1823 and 1857, members of the Batt family were responsible for running a private madhouse, which was opened in April 1823. *Jackson's Oxford Journal* for 12 April carries the following advertisement for it: 'To Parents and Guardians: Edward Batt, surgeon etc, having been solicited to open a house for the reception of persons labouring under diseases of the mind, begs to state that he has now accommodation for patients of that description near to his residence, in Witney, Oxfordshire. Terms and other particulars may be known on application to him.'

The madhouse was established at No 33 High Street, the site on which the present Congregational Church stands. It was licensed to receive 20 patients, though numbers never exceeded 16, mostly women. There were probably never more than four male patients at one time. The sexes did not meet, for the men's and women's quarters were separated by two boundary walls more than ten feet high.

A family business established in the first half of the 19th century was that of the Clarkes, ironmongers in the High Street. The firm was started by Thomas Clarke, born in July 1813. As a young man he had been employed by Mr Clarke Hartley, who worked on the fitting-out of Clinch's Brewery. In 1839 Hartley's business was taken over by Messrs Staple and Lea, and Thomas Clarke set up on his own in Corn Street, doing general tinsmith work. In 1863 he moved to larger premises in the High Street, part of which had been the male wing of the madhouse. The shop is still there, under the same name, though the Clarke family no longer own it. Old Thomas Clarke must have been skilled with his hands, for he was reputed to be able to make a complete miniature tea service out of a five-shilling piece.

Ironmongery seems to be a trade that remains in the family for several generations: Leigh's of Market Square is another example of a business going back to the early 19th century. The firm was founded by Samuel Lea, born in 1801. During the 19th century it expanded to include iron founding, corn milling at Farm Mill and the sale and repair of farm implements, and during the early part of the 20th century there was a petrol pump outside the shop. Samuel Lea took as his apprentice Alfred Lea Leigh, so called because his mother, Samuel Lea's sister, had married Thomas Leigh of Swindon. All his children used the name Lea Leigh.

The building trade has always been important to Witney. In the Victorian period the architecture of the town was very much the responsibility of two brothers, George (1813-1890) and William Wilkinson (1819-1901). George's most important contribution was the construction of the Workhouse in 1836. It stood on the street that later became known as Tower Hill. During the Second World War the building was taken over by Crawford Collets Ltd. Most of the original Workhouse has now been demolished.

William Wilkinson was, as far as Witney goes, a far more prolific builder than his brother. He was responsible for the first police station (1860), near the entrance to Henry Box School, as well as the two chapels and the lodge at the cemetery (1857), and the almshouses in Saint Mary's churchyard. At the age of 38 he left Witney to live in Oxford, where he designed many public buildings, including the Randolph Hotel. One of his specialities was the design of model farm buildings: many of his Gothic farm cottages can be seen around Witney.

Most of the mills in Witney, as we know them today, are the work of a local builder-cum-architect, William Cantwell. The latter half of the 19th century brought the modernisaton of the weaving process from hand looms to power looms which, of course, needed to be housed in mills rather than in cottages and weaving sheds. It was Cantwell who did most of this work. He re-designed New Mill after its destruction by fire in 1883, and supervised the improvements and additions to it throughout the decade. Witney Mill in Mill Street was also his work, as was William Smith's mill in Bridge Street. One of his buildings was the Newland Warehouse: it is now gone for ever, for a huge fire destroyed it in 1975, and the remains had to be demolished.

Though many of the important buildings in the town were designed by either the Wilkinson brothers or William Cantwell, the main builders were Bartlett Brothers Ltd, in the High Street. The firm was started by Malachi Bartlett, who settled in Witney in about 1836, and lived at 37 West End. He started working with James Long, and helped with the building of the 1850 Wesleyan Chapel in the High Street. By 1852 Bartlett had established his own business with his son Christopher, at 94 High Street. Later, they moved to larger premises at Nos 71 and 73, afterwards acquiring 75 as well. Like all old Witney properties, each of these buildings had a considerable amount of land, so that the Bartletts had room to develop a large construction company. They installed a steam-driven saw and machine shop; they burned their own bricks and had a lime-kiln. Many of their Witney buildings were made of stone; to supply this they had their own quarries, employing no fewer than 50 men.

Witney has always been well-endowed with inns and ale-houses. In the 19th century, when the population was less than 6,000, there were over 30 inns, most of which still exist today. The brewing of ale started as soon as the town was founded: one of the rights granted by the Bishops of Winchester to the citizens of all their new towns was to hold the assize of bread and ale. This meant that the town could appoint its own inspector to check on the quality of all beer brewed there.

At first, the brewing of beer was a small-scale affair, with most inns and many households brewing their own. Then, during the 19th century, the idea of tied inns gradually spread. Brewing became more centralised, purpose-built breweries were established and their owners bought up inns, which then sold only their special brand of beer. In Witney, this important industry was carried on by three major breweries.

The largest and the longest-lived was Clinch's Eagle Brewery. The first hint of the involvement of the Clinch family in brewing is when James Clinch, son of John Clinch the banker, bought the Fleece Inn in 1811. Witney parish register for 1820 refers to James Clinch as a 'brewer/woolstapler', and Piggot's Directory for 1823 describes him as a maltster. During the 1830s, several cottages west of Church Green were demolished to make way for the new Clinch's Brewery. The scale of the 19th century business can be judged from the fact that in 1891 Clinch's owned 72 tied public houses scattered between Oxford and Swindon. The brewery continued to function until 1962, when it was taken over by Courage's, and in 1963 brewing stopped. The building became a supply depot. Even this ceased in 1978, and most of the brewery was pulled down, the site becoming a small industrial estate. However, in 1982 a new brewery started up, using the old maltings area of the Eagle site, so the tradition has not been lost.

Clinch's greatest rival was the Blanket Hall Brewery, started some time after 1844 by William Smith, the founder of Bridge Street Mills, in collaboration with Joseph Early. 1844 was the year when the Blanket Company, its relevance to modern blanket-making gone, sold the Hall, 'with the kitchens, outhouses, yard and garden', for £200 to Edward Early, the blanket manufacturer. In the outbuildings was the brewing plant, complete with casks, which had been used to provide refreshment at the many meetings and feasts of the Blanket Company. This seemed to Edward Early an excellent opportunity for his son Joseph and William Smith to set up a brewery. The original plant had a capacity of 12 bushels, which the two partners expanded; but when the question of how the expansion was to be paid for arose, they could not agree. The partnership broke up. William Smith carried on alone, and expanded the business still further.

His lease on the Blanket Hall was only a yearly one, and Edward Early gave him notice to quit. According to William this was a move to try to restore the partnership, as business by this time was profitable. However, he felt that he was not getting a good enough deal, and moved all his brewing plant to Bridge Street, where he set up the White Hart Brewery. This establishment was still working in 1854, but probably came to an end soon after that, as William became more and more involved in the mop-making business.

Joseph Early continued to brew beer at the Blanket Hall, but by 1869 the brewery was operated by the Shillingford brothers, and another change of management is shown in *Kelly's Directory* of 1881, which lists Arthur Bateman of the Blanket Hall Brewery. By this time it must have been quite a large business for, when Clinch's bought it out in 1890, it owned 23 tied houses. After the takeover, the Blanket Hall Brewery buildings were used by the company of Dale and Sharpe as a mineral water factory, which operated until the Second World War.

William Gillett, a member of the banking family, was another Witney citizen attracted to brewing. In 1860 he was running the Britannia Brewery in the square behind the Corn Exchange. This brewery traded until 1875, when it was sold. The notice of sale described it as 'consisting of a brewhouse, workroom, 2 hop rooms over and all necessary appliance for carrying on a 20 bushel brewery'. Besides the brewery there were four public houses: the Eagle and the Chequers in Corn Street, the Lamb in Crawley, and the Strickland Arms in Ducklington. All these public houses were bought by Hunt's Brewery of Bicester, who had an agency and a small brewery at the Eagle Vaults. There were several other small breweries in the town, the most important being run by Thomas Hains in Corn Street.

During the 19th century the grocery trade was important. One business from those times which still flourishes is that of Saltmarsh and Druce of Market Square.

There were many small groceries dotted about the town, but the most prominent business was Tarrant and Sons, of 32 and 36 Market Square. The shop was started in 1832 by Mr Warrington, who had a public house demolished in order to build it. In about 1840 the business was run by Edgar Smith, and in 1851 it was taken over by William Tarrant, who greatly expanded it to include the Corn Street Stores and a shop in West End. Tarrant's was a wholesale as well as a retail business. It even had a banana-ripening room, built in 1907. On the night of the coronation of George V a fire broke out in the shop, causing so much damage that it was not able to reopen until about a year later, in April 1912. In 1919 the Market Square shop was sold to Percy Bartlett. After other changes the building was sold for re-development in 1960, and is now the site of a retail shop.

The nearest thing to a department store in 19th century Witney was Valentine and Barrell, who advertised themselves as tailors, drapers and furniture dealers. Their main shop was in the centre of Market Square, on the site which is now a café. They also traded from 23, 25, 29 and 31 Market Square. In 1898 A.E. Barrell bought the patent name 'The Witney Blanket Company' from the drapers Fred Clapper and Co, and set up a mail order business in connection with the firm of Valentine and Barrell. In 1913 this company had its headquarters at 39 and 41 Market Square. New premises were built on The Leys in 1920, only to be destroyed by fire in 1921. They were rebuilt, and trading went on until 1933, when Barrell sold out to Henry Ltd, who continued to run a mail order business.

Another shop of importance in the late Victorian era and on into the 20th century was Cook and Boggis, Cash Drapers and Clothiers, Wholesale and Retail, of 3 Market Square. Fire, a potent force in the commercial history of Witney, struck on 12 December 1964, destroying the building. A new supermarket, Waitrose, was built on the site. In its turn, this was partly demolished in the mid-1980s to form the entrance to the new Woolgate shopping centre and Waitrose complex.

There was something for everybody in enterprising 19th century Witney. As well as these large businesses, there were many smaller ones, like George Williams of Corn Street, a birdcage maker. When the occupant of the cage succumbed to old age, its grieving owner could always call upon the skill of William Ball, Hairdresser and Taxidermist, of Wood Green on the other side of town. Though there was no great need to go shopping in Oxford, those who enjoyed a change of scene found the train journey an easy one, especially as they could be met by Mr Payne's horse-drawn bus on their parcel-laden return.

In the past the production of blankets and other woven cloth was Witney's biggest and best-known industry, but it was not the only one. After all, Witney was a market town serving a large agricultural community, and therefore much of its industry was based on the needs of the farmers.

There were several blacksmiths and farriers in the town, as well as wagon and coach builders and agricultural implement repairers. The blacksmiths were also able to repair the steam engines when they were introduced into the woollen mills. Tanning and glove making were two more 19th century industries: the glove making was very much a cottage industry, requiring no machinery.

It was not until the Second World War that new industry came, in the form of the de Havilland Company, which set up an aircraft repair unit in the old Witney Aerodrome. At its peak the company employed 1,200 people. Its presence meant that the blanket industry was no longer the only large employer of local labour, and also that new and useful skills were introduced to the area. De Havilland remained in Witney until August 1949, when the company returned to its factory at Leavesden in Hertfordshire.

The site of the old aerodrome was sold to Smith's of England, who transferred their motor accessories division there, and set up the manufacture of motor car heaters. It was to become the largest employer in the area, with the exception of Morris Cars at Cowley, which later became British Leyland. A writer in the *Witney Gazette*, describing the 1950s, says 'Though few people realised it at the time, Witney's years as an insular, self-contained community had ended, and the town was jet-propelled into the 20th century.'

During its first 30 years, the company produced 24 million car heaters. It diversified into various groups: as well as the car heater plant there were Smith's Hydraulics, which came to Witney in 1957, and Precision Fans, which started in 1967 and made fans for such diverse items as air-conditioning units and photocopying machines.

All this industrial expansion meant that new housing was urgently needed. The first new estate was built by the Windrush Valley Housing Association in the 1950s, to cater for the newly imported labour for Smith's Industries. This was not a popular move with some of the old-established residents, who found it hard to accept so many newcomers all at once.

An industry that provided numerous jobs in Witney was Bowyer's (Wiltshire) Ltd, which operated a factory in Corn Street. Its origins go back to Percy Bartlett, who made his own sausages on his Market Square premises between 1928 and 1933. After selling his shop he had a small factory built at 79 High Street, and another in Gloucester Place. He started to act as distributor for Brazil's (of Amersham, Bucks) cooked meat, and this larger company bought him out in 1934. Brazil's built the Corn Street works in 1947, and was itself taken over by Bowyer's in 1970. Later, Bowyer's was taken over by Northern Foods, which closed its Witney branch in 1990.

Witney's modern expansion dates from the early 1950s. Then, it was a small market town of under 6,000 people, relying on one industry. Now, in 1994, the population has risen to nearly 20,000, and is still growing. Although Smith's Industries has contracted with the decline in the fortunes of the car industry, many new enterprises have sprung up in several new industrial estates, some of which, appropriately, have been set up on old blanket mill premises.

Local enterprise finds a showcase every two years in the Witney Trade Fair, organised by the Chamber of Trade. This event takes place in and around a huge marquee on Church Green, and provides four days of bustling activity for residents and thousands of visitors, as well as the opportunity to display the goods and skills on offer in this part of Oxfordshire.

Clinch's Eagle Brewery, 1939.

The beer cellar at Clinch's Eagle Brewery, 1939
–'its sole constituents are pure water, malt, hops and yeast... and if any man would tell you that any... chemicals are added you may give him the lie, for there is certainly no brewery in England that would sink to such measure.'

Dale & Sharpe's soda water factory, set up in the Blanket Hall after the Blanket Hall Brewery closed down.

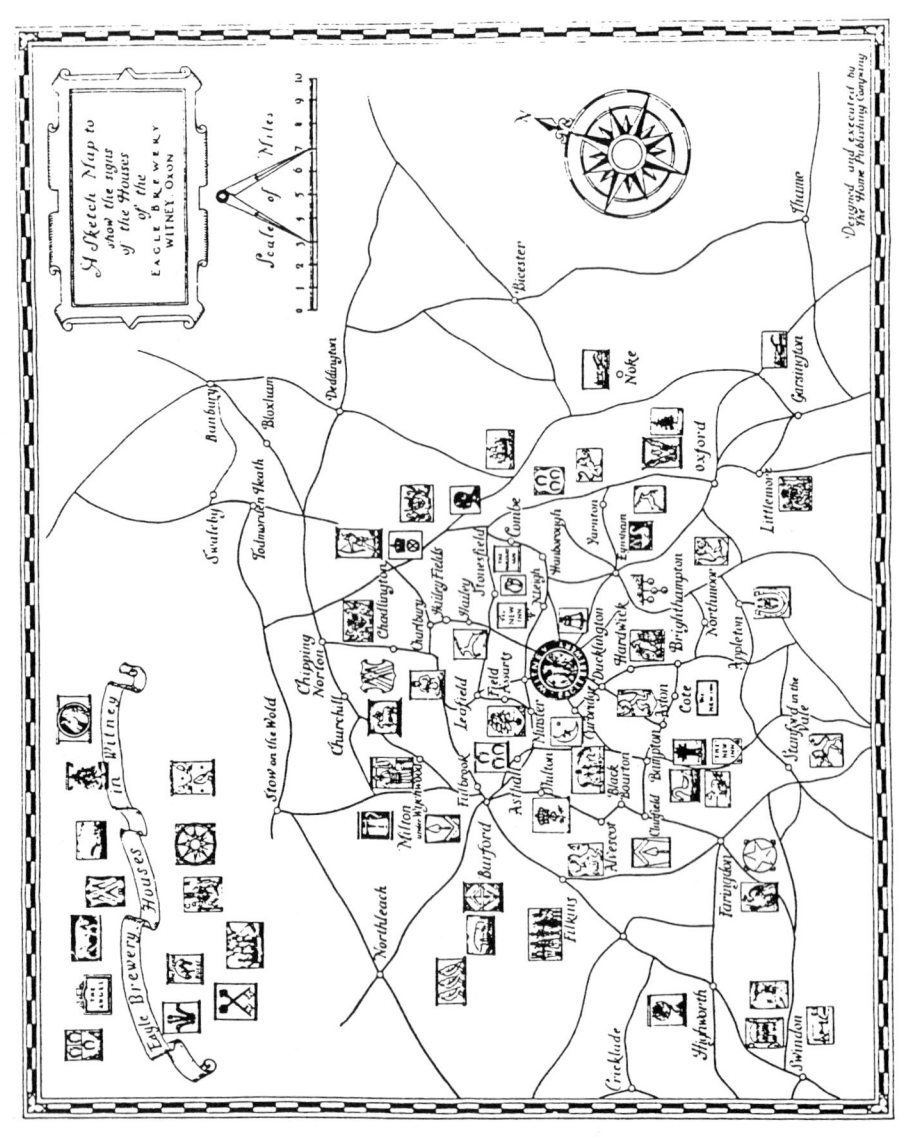

'A Pictorial Map Showing the Area covered by Clinch & Co Ltd's Eagle Brewery Witney' 1939.

Xmas 19*15*.

Mr Barratt
Ducklington
Dr. to

A. E. HORNE,

CORN, CAKE, SEED and MANURE MERCHANT,

156, 158, 160, Corn Street,

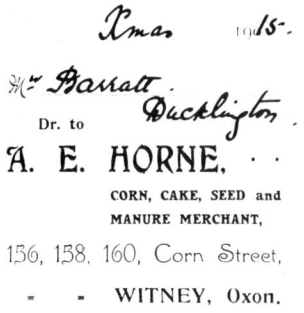

- - WITNEY, Oxon.

Agent for Holland & Coombe's Cake & Calf Meal.

All Kinds of Artificial Manures.

Seeds of every Description.

A. E. Horne, Corn, Cake, Seed and Manure Merchant, Xmas 1915 (OMS Acc 85.105.1)

156, 158, 160 Corn Street, 1986. (CG)

The corner of Corn Street and Market Square, C1830, showing the Red Lion, which still exists, and the Lamb and Flag, which does not. Drawn by W. Seely.

The same corner, c1845. (OMS: 85.105.1)

The Corn Street/Market Square corner showing Tarrants shop decked out for George V's jubilee, 1935. (TW)

The same corner in 1985. Tarrant's shop was demolished in 1960. (CG)

R. A. Jones, Est 1840, specialised in cabinet making, upholstery and house clearance. The cottages on the right were demolished in the 1960s to make way for Holloway Road. (CW)

They later moved across the road to No. 43 Corn Street, where the firm still sells furniture. (CW)

Leigh & Sons. Note the early petrol pump on the pavement outside. (TW)

Leigh's Warehouse in Marlborough Lane. (TW)

The 'Elizabethan House' drawn by W. Seely, c1850

Richard Berry Hobbs' glass and china shop in the 'Elizabethan' House, with the Witney Coffee Tavern opposite, 1887. (OCL)

The Corn Returns Office, on the site of the present Corn Exchange which was built in 1856, drawn by W. Seely.

All these buildings drawn by W. Seely have been pulled down to make way for the Co-op.

EPILOGUE 1994

In October 1945 the Witney Debating Society met at the Town Hall to try to answer the question, 'Whither Witney?' posed by S.P.B. Mais in an *Oxford Mail* article of 10 September.

Members' hopes for the future were fairly modest and eminently practical. One said that the bus company should organise a good service, with buses fitting in for transport around the district. There should be 'a good bus centre, for passengers and staff'. He thought that an early service by diesel train would be useful. The town also needed an 'indoor swimming bath and washing bath', and a public library and reading room. Catering establishments should serve more 'good honest country food', and the market should be open daily to sell farm produce. Another member spoke up for an adequate housing scheme, light industries, proper sewerage, adequate entertainment, playgrounds, and a health centre.

Now, in the 1990s, there is no longer a Witney Debating Society, though there is no shortage of opinions or chances to express them. The transport-minded member would probably be quite pleased with the buses now, for there are frequent double-decker and minibus services to Oxford, linking with coaches to London. There are local minibuses connecting the town centre with the outlying estates and villages. The 'good bus centre' has not materialised, however. As for the trains, they run only in the memory of long-term Witney residents. Youngsters - and newer arrivals, like the writers of this book - just have to use their imagination.

The indoor swimming-bath certainly exists. It is part of a large and expanding sports complex also containing squash courts, which would probably surprise the 1945 debaters. There is not, however, a 'washing bath', but nobody complains, as houses without bathrooms are almost unheard-of nowadays.

The public library on the 1960s Welch Way development, with its children's section and reading room, is handy for the town centre. Nearby there are two health centres, and even a community hospital, which opened in April 1981.

'Good honest country food' is certainly available to the Witney diner-out at various restaurants and public houses, as well as modern 'fast food' and more sophisticated international dishes. In addition, there are Chinese and Indian restaurants, a development which could hardly have been predicted in 1945. The market is still only twice weekly, however, and modern farm production and distribution methods do not encourage the sale of local produce.

Shopping in the 1990s is very different from shopping at the end of the Second World War, in Witney as in any other town. Supermarkets belonging to huge national chains display kinds and quantities of foodstuffs beyond the wildest dreams of the 1945 housewife, dominated by shortages and rationing. A large new shopping centre has been built on the old burgage plots near the Windrush, where Witney citizens once grew cabbages and kept pigs. However, the traditional Thursday and Saturday markets still provide a much-appreciated service to people in the town and the surrounding villages. On those days, the Welch Way and Waitrose car parks, which are large, open and free of charge, are usually packed. The car owners make for the market, the supermarkets, the banks and the public houses, one of which, in the days before unrestricted daytime opening hours, was allowed to stay open all day on market days, as inns close to markets traditionally had the right to do. So, although the market is quite small, it plays an important part in the life of the town.

The 1945 debater who was concerned about housing would find that a large number of estates have been built, both Council and private. Witney has been scheduled as a 'growth town' by the West Oxfordshire District Council. The population in 1945 was under 6,000; now it is expected to rise to over 20,000 by 1995. He also felt that light industry would benefit the town. This has arrived, and discreetly occupies an industrial estate on the site of the old railway station, as well as smaller ones on Bridge Street, West End, the old Eagle Brewery site and others. Sewerage fortunately seems to pose no problem nowadays.

Nothing very startling has happened on the entertainment scene. There are plenty of public houses, but then there always were. Various clubs and societies cater for many age-groups, interests and sports, though probably no more than there were in the self-sufficient 1940s. There are sports fields, children's playgrounds and hard tennis courts. Dances, concerts by local choirs and musicians, as well as Witney Dramatic Society productions, take place at the Corn Exchange or the Langdale Hall, but the Palace Cinema, after years of struggle, has finally closed down. However, the Corn Exchange now provides a venue for regular film shows.

Town twinning has come to Witney: its opposite numbers are Le Touquet on the coast of Northern France and Unterhaching, near Munich. This recent development has led to interesting cultural and social exchanges between the towns.

Travel has grown in importance in Witney just as it has everywhere else: the number of travel agents operating in the town is proof of this. A less beguiling aspect is the traffic queue which toils its way along the A40 to Oxford every morning. S.P.B. Mais's article in 1945 mentioned that 'about 150 men go to Oxford daily, to Morris and elsewhere'. Those 150, now honourably retired, or sadly deceased, have been replaced by many hundreds of men and women who go by car or bus to work in Oxford's shops, offices, factories and colleges. The rush-hour journey in has few attractions, but coming back, once the big roundabouts of Oxford are behind you, is a different story. From the top of Oxford Hill you can see Witney serenely spread out before you, a comforting sight after a hard day. But be careful - there is a 30 mph sign halfway down the hill. You must slow down a little before you come into Witney. Take your time, and enjoy it. There is nowhere else like it.

Witney Trade Fair, June 1994. (JG)

BIBLIOGRAPHY

A. Ballard, The Black Death in Witney, *Oxford Archaeological Society Report*, 1909.

M. Bee, Clinch and Company, Brewers: an Oxfordshire Business History, *Oxfordshire Local History*, vol 2, No 2.

J.L. Bolton and M.M. Maslen, Calendar of the Court Books of the Borough of Witney, 1538-1610, *Oxfordshire Record Society*, vol LIV, 1985.

C.J. Bond, The Origins of Witney, *Record of Witney*, vols 3, 4, 1978.

T.J. Cooper, Aspects of the Old Poor Law in Witney, 1536-1834, *Record of Witney*, vol 12.

R.E. Early, *Apprentice*, R.K.P. 1977.

M. Fleming, *Witney Grammar School, 1660-1960*.

M. Gelling, *The Place-names of Oxfordshire*, 1953.

J.A. Giles, *History of Witney*, 1852.

G.B. Grundy, Saxon Charters of Oxfordshire, *Oxfordshire Record Society*, XV, 1933.

P. Hyde, 'The Borough of Witney', Oxfordshire Hundred Rolls of 1279, *Oxfordshire Record Society*, XLVI, 1968.

P. Hyde, *The Winchester Manors of Witney and Adderbury, Oxfordshire*, B. Litt. thesis, 1954, Bodleian Library, B. Litt. d. 473.

S.C. Jenkins, Some Thoughts on the Topography of Saxon Witney, *Record of Witney*, vol 12.

S.C. Jenkins, *The Witney and East Gloucester Railway*, 1974.

W.J. Monk, *History of Witney*, 1894.

W.Ll. Parry-Jones, *The Trade in Lunacy: A Study of Private Madhouses in England in the Eighteenth and Nineteenth Centuries*.

A. Plummer and R. Early, *The Blanket Makers*, R.K.P. 1969.

A. Plummer, *The Witney Blanket Industry*, George Routledge, 1934.

K. Rodwell, *Historic Towns of Oxfordshire*, Oxfordshire Archaeological Unit.

J. Sherwood and N. Pevsner, *The Buildings of England: Oxfordshire*.

C. Smith, *Two Men's Ministries*, 1983.

F. Woodward, *Oxfordshire Parks*, Oxfordshire Museum Services, 1982.

A. Young, *A General View of the Agriculture of Oxfordshire*, 1809.

Oldfield, *Calendar of Oxon Quarter Session Rolls*, 1687-1830, OCRO.

Calendar of State Papers, PRO.

Registers of Baptism, Marriage and Burial, OCRO.
Witney Tithe Award, OCRO.
Churchwardens' Accounts, 1569-1720, D.D. Par Witney, OCRO.
Vestry Minute Book, 1793-1823, D.D. Par Witney, OCRO.
Papers concerning Witney Charities, D.D. Par Witney, OCRO.
Report of the Charity Commissioners, 1822, 1882, OCRO.
Annual Reports of the Medical Officer of Health for Witney Urban and Rural Sanitary Authority, 1893-1920, OCRO.

D.A.E. Cross, Notes on the History of Witney, OCL.

Unpublished papers concerning the Batt family in the possession of Captain and Mrs A.H. Swann, Burford.

Unpublished autobiography of William Smith, in the possession of D. Smith, High Cogges.

Witney Gazette; Witney Express; Oxford Mail; Jackson's Oxford Journal; Record of Witney, vols 1-19; Oxfordshire Trade Directories, and Witney Census Returns.

Key to Caption Credits

OMS	Oxfordshire Museum Services
OCL	Oxfordshire County Library
OAU	Oxford Archaeological Unit
PRO	Public Record Office
AshM	Ashmolean Museum
WTC	Witney Town Council
BL	Bodleian Library
OM	Oxford Mail
E	Early's of Witney, PLC
TW	Tom Worley
KS	Kate Steane
SJ	Stanley Jenkins
DD	John Dossett-Davies
AT	Arthur Titherington
RA	Richard Adams
CG	Charles Gott
JG	Joan Gott
CW	Carol and David Wilcox
BC	Brian Crawford

INDEX

A40......14,22,86,132
Airfield 94,96,99,104,119
Air raid (precautions)...95,96
Akeman Street....15
Alfred, son of Queen Emma................19
almshouses 28,33,35,115
Alresford........101
Alvescot............29
American servicemen........94
Anabaptists.......70
Apley Barn.......103
d'Arsic, Robert...21
Ashcombe, Richard 29,36
Ashfield, Hannah 113
Asthall..............15
Attwell, John......30
Baker, John........69
Ball, William.....118
Bampton......17,29
Bands
Brize Norton.....96
Temperance......79
Town..........79,96
Banks
Barclay's........113
Batt's.............113
Birmingham Banking Co.....113
Gillett & Clinch 113
Gillett & Co 110,113
Metropolitan..113
Midland..........113
Witney & Oxfordshire.....112
Barford.............47
Barker, Hugh......29
Barrell, A.E.......118
Bartlett
Brothers Ltd...115
Christopher....115
Malachi........115
Percy......118,119
Bateman, Arthur 117
Batt
family...41,73,113
Augustine William 113
Dr Charles
Dorrington 41,113
Edward........113
House............42

Belgian Refugees 93,94
Birmingham.......86
Bishops
Bancroft..........64
Fell................70
Secker............70
Wilberforce......65
Bishop's Palace 16,20,23,24,25,26,91
Black Death...22,111
Blackwell Hall.....85
Bladon..............85
Blake,
Francis.......69,70
William........36,40 66,69,70
Blanket
Company...51,102 116,118
Charter..........54
Hall 40,50,51,52, 60,116,117,121
Blankets 47,48,49,51 52,53,56,57,118
Bolton, Edward...32
bombs............95
Boots the Chemist 75
Borough Court 101,102
Bourton on the Water...............93
Bowyer's (Wiltshire) Ltd...........119,120
Box family 37,38,112
Henry......30,37,39
Mary...............37
Philip..........29,30
Brabant, John.....69
Brampton, Moses 64
bread and beef houses.......28,34,35
Breakspear, Martha 30
Breweries
Blanket Hall 116,117
Britannia........117
Clinch's 114,116,117
Courage's.......116
Eagle..116,120,121, 122,131
Eagle Vaults....117
Hunts............117
White Hart......117
Brice family......23
Stephen..........29

Bridewell..........32
bridge.........84,108
Brightwell..........48
Bristol Fighters...94
British Leyland..119
Bronze Age.....14,15
Buckshell, John..113
Burford..14,29,48,93
Burford-Campsfield Road Trust.........86
Butter Cross.......36
Butter Cross Works 53
Calais.............112
Canadian servicemen 94
canals...............86
Canterbury Archbishop of 19,20,91
Cantwell, William 115
carillon..............66
Carter, Edward....29
Cassington.........86
Castleton..........29
Caswell.............91
Chamber of Trade 120
Charity Commissioners 18,29,30,31,38,39,40
Charlbury Roads Trust................86
Charles Early & Marriott (Witney) Limited.............53
charters 13,17,18,49, 101
Churches and Chapels
Cogges.....69,108
Congregational 73,74,114
chapel in the burial ground......73,115
Davenport Road 74
Friends' Meeting House........68,69
Holy Trinity 65,67,78
Our Lady and St Hugh.........72,74
Primitive Methodist 74
St Mary the Virgin 28,62,63,64,65,

69,78,87,95
Wenman.........41
Wesleyan 71,72,115
Welcome Evangelical.....75
workhouse chapel 72
Church Commissioners...78
cinema..79,83,95,131
Civil Defence...95,96
Civil War........92,93
Clapper, Fred & Co 118
Clarendon, Earl of 23,49
Clarke
family..........114
Thomas....77,114
Clinch
family. 113,116,117
James......113,116
John.....32,113,116
John Williams..113
William.........113
Coffee Tavern 79,128
Cogges
13,18,20,21,33,36,40, 66,69,70,91,105
Farm Museum..56
Wood............80
Cokethorpe Park..87
Collier family 52,112
Robert............32
Commonwealth 23,79,93
Company of Witney Blanket Weavers 49,51,60
Congregationalists 64,69,70
Convent of Sisters of Charity.......41,72
Cook & Boggis...118
Cook, Thomas.....32
Co-op, The........129
Cork, James........30
Cornbury, Lord...23
Corn Exchange 79,80,95,105,106,117, 129,131
Corn Returns Office 129
Corn Street Stores 117
Costell, Thomas...85

135

Index

Cotswold Hills 13,14,47
Council Offices....95
County Council 38,41
Cowley............119
Crawford Collets 33,114
Crawley............17
Cromwell, Oliver..93
Crutchfield, Richard 69,70
Cunningham, Francis Macaulay....64,65,78
Curbridge..17,29,33, 102
Curbridge Down 77,80
D-Day..............95
Dale & Sharpe 117,121
Danes.............19
de Haviland 96,99,119
Devil's Quoits......14
Diver, Thomas.....33
Domesday Book 13,19
Down-towns.......78
Dramatic Society 80,131
Drill Hall.....95,100
Dudley, Sir Andrew 23
duffles............48
Early family.. 52,53
  Charles William 55,59
  Edward. 52,116,117
  John..............51
  Joseph..30,116,117
  Richard...........61
  T. and W........105
  Thomas......30,39
Early's Blanket Factory.......18,53,60
East Ward........101
Edgerley, William 29
Edwards, William 64
Elizabethan House.............128
Em's Ditch..14,15,18
enclosures......91,92
evacuees from London..80,93,94,95
Eynsham 21,29,30,52,72,85,86
  Abbey.........21,72
  Abbot of......... 21
  fairs..........21,22,77
  Fairford............87

Farnham..........101
Fawler..............92
Feast, Witney 76,77,82
Fermor, Thomas 111
Field House....... 73
Fifield..............29
Fire Service..105,106, 107
Fire Station 105,106, 109
flying shuttle....... 61
Football Club, Witney............80
Foxley Norris, Rev W. 78
Freeland.....29,30
  charity.....29,30,31
  Freind, Rev Robert 40,62,70
  Friends, Society of 69
  fulling mills.19,20,21, 47,48
  fulling stocks.......57
  Gardener, William 32
  George, John......52
  German aircraft... 97
  German POWs....94
  Gilbert's Act, 1782 33
  Giles, Rev Dr J.H 18,77
Gillett,
  Alfred...........113
  Charles..........113
  William.......117
  golf................80
  Goole, John, BA...37
  grain, price of.......92
  Grand Union Canal 86
  Gray, Lord......... 91
  Great Western Railway......86,87
  Green, Elizabeth..29
Gregory,
  Dr Francis.......70
  Thomas...........70
  Grocers Company 37,38
  Gune, William.....69
  Gunne family 93,112
  Hailey 17,22,33,39,69, 91,102
  Hains, Thomas...117
  Hampton Gay......91
Harcourt,
  Earl of........... 60
  John (gent)...... 91
Harris,

Ada Leonora.... 11
Charles............11
John............. 69
Maria............11
Paul.............51
Hart,
  John.............69
  Kester...........69
Hartley, Clarke...114
Hartshorn, Daniel 32
Haynes, James.....30
Hayter, Mr.........94
Henry Ltd........118
High Cogges........40
Hill, The............41
History of Witney 13,18,77
Hobbes, Richard Berry..............128
Holloway, John 28,33,34,38,39
Holway Grange....29
Home Guard.......96
Horne, A.E., Corn, Cake, Seed and Manure Merchants 123
Howes, William...49
Hudson's Bay Company.......48,52
Hundred Rolls 21,22,77
Hurricanes.........96
Independents..69,70
Indians, North American......... 48
Inns and public houses
  Angel............80
  Black Horse..... 81
  Blue Boar........85
  Bull..............80
  Chequers.......117
  Court........... 85
  Crown Hotel 85,89
  Czar of Russia.. 93
  Eagle........... 117
  Fleece Inn......116
  House of Windsor 93
  King of Prussia..93
  Kings Head...... 85
  Lamb, Crawley 117
  Lamb and Flag 124
  Marlborough Arms 85,113
  Red Lion....... 124
  Staple Hall ..34,51, 52,85,87,89,101

Strickland Arms, Ducklington....117
Three Horseshoes 81
White Hart 44,79, 93
Iron Age.....13,14,15
Jackson's Oxford Journal............113
James, Henry......29
Jerram, Charles...65
Jones, R.A........126
jousts...............77
Jubilee plaque.....45
Kay, John..........56
Kelly's Directory, 1881.............117
Kings
  Canute...........19
  Charles I......92,93
  Edgar........13,17
  Edward the Confessor.....18,19
  Edward IV.......32
  Edward VI.......23
  Ethelred the Unready..........19
  George V..118,125
  Hardicanute.....19
  Henry III....21,22, 47,77
  John..........21,26
  Stephen.......20,91
Kneller, Sir Godfrey 60
Langdale Hall 95,100,131
Langel Common 108
Langley.........17,21
Lea, Samuel.......114
Lea Leigh, Alfred 114
Lechlade...........86
Leigh family 114,127
  Thomas.........114
  & Sons..........127
Lenthall, William 23,93
Le Touquet.......131
Levellers...........93
Leys, The...62,76,77, 78,94,118
Local Boards.....102
Local Defence Volunteers.........96
local government 101,102
Local Government Act, 1863..........102

INDEX

London and North Western Railway..86
Long, James......115
Long Parliament..23
Longworth.........37
loom,
  hand......56,61,115
  power........57,115
Lords, House of...49
madhouse 73,113,114
Mais, S.P.B..130,132
market, Thursday 22,131
Marlborough, Duke of....................23
Marriott family 52,53
Marriotts Close...80
Martin, John.......29
Mather, Rev Samuel 69
Maud, Richard....64
Merchandise Marks Act..................53
Methodists........71
Middle Ward.....101
milestone..........87
Mills
  Bridge Street 60,77,105,116
  Butter Cross Works 53
  Charles Early and Marriott..........53
  Collier's..........55
  Farm Mill....19,114
  Fawler.............92
  New Mill 51,78,115
  Walker's.........53
  William Smith 53,115
  Witney Mill..19,59, 107,115
  Woodford Mill...18
Millin's Yard.....105
Minchin, Thomas 69
Monk, Rev W.J. 13,18,64,78,105
Mop Fair...........77
mop-making..48,105
Morris Cars..119,132
Mount House......87
Napoleonic Wars..51
National School Movement.........40
Natural History Society..............78
Neolithic...........14
Newland 21,40,59, 61,86,88,105,107

Warehouse.....115
Newlands, Eynsham 21
Newsham, Yorks..20
Newtown, IOW..101
Nonconformists 41,69,70,93,102
Norman Conquest 91
Normans........19,91
Northern Foods..120
Northleach.........85
North Leigh....15,92
Northumberland, Duke of............23
Norton, Silas.......69
Oelfhelm, thegn 13,17,18,24
Oriel College, Oxford 37
Oxford..29,30,32,85, 92,93,113,115, 118,130,132
Oxfordshire and Buckinghamshire Light Infantry......96
Oxford Canal......86
Oxford Mail...96,130
Oxford, Worcester and Wolverhampton Railway............87
Oxford University Golf Club...........80
Palmer, John......29
Parkinson, John...69
Parliament.........22
Parmo, Thomas...30
Partridge, James...64
Paternoster.....69
Ward............101
Payne (carrier)...118
Penn, William.....69
Penny family......112
Philips (Yorkshire blanket company) 53
Pickersgill, Miss...80
Piggot's Directory, 1823...............116
pike house, Church Lane..........86,88
plague..............22
Plot, Dr Robert....50
Plummer, Alfred 48,51
Police Station 95,105, 115
Poor Laws.....29,102
Portuguese workers 72,94

Prayer Book Rebels 91
Presbyterians......70
Pritchard's Glove Works....... 105,107
Protestants.........69
Quakers........ 69,70
Queens
  Anne.........49,60
  Elizabeth the Queen Mother..39
  Emma........ 18,19
  Mary.............23
  Matilda, Empress 20,91
RAF.................96
Randolph Hotel..115
Rectory............ 62
repertory company 80
Restoration.........23
Rifle Corps........ 93
Riot Act............92
Rochester, Earl of 23
Rodda, Richard....71
Roddy, Father John 72
Roman Catholics 41,72
Romans.....14,15,18
Rowe, John........79
Royal Flying Corps 94
Royal Ordnance Papers.............92
Royal Pipe Rolls 1179 47
Royalists........ 92,93
Rylands and Sons 53
Saltmarsh & Druce 80,117
Savory, Thomas...30
Saxons..13,18,27,63, 91
Saxon Charter.....17
Schools
  Ashford Grammar 95
  Batt School...41,55
  Blue Coat.... 33,38, 39,40,41,52
  dame school, Bridge Street 52,70
  Grammar School 30,37,38,40,42,43, 70,95,112
  Henry Box .. 33,39, 62,95,105,115

National School, Bridge Street 40,41,44
National School, Church Green 40,93
Our Lady of Lourdes...... 41,72
Quaker School 41
St Mary's 40,46
Technical School 38
Wesleyan School 41,45,46
Wesleyan Sunday School............ 41
West End (Anglican)....... 40
Wood Green.... 39
Sharpe, Elizabeth .29
sheep................47
Sheppard, Thomas 29
Shillingford Brothers 117
Shipton............. 29
Smith, Edgar...117
Henry.............52
Herbert........105
Humphrey... 63,64
William 40,52,53,60 77,78,105,116,117
Smith's
Blankets.....44,53
Estate............ 22
Hydraulics.....119
Industries 94, 119,120
Mills.........53,105
Smithman, Edward 77,78
Sopwith Pups......94
South Leigh...70,113
Spitfires............96
Spittle, Richard....33
Stanton Harcourt 14,79
Staple and Lea....114
Staple Hall.........34
station.. 76,87,97,131
steeplechases......77
Steere, Barth.....91
John.............91
Stonesfield.....39,64
Streets, etc
Bridge Street 40,44,52,53,93, 115,117,131
Burford Road 77

INDEX

Church Green 33,35,37,40,41,46, 62,76,77,80,94,95, 96,101,103,116, 120
Church Lane 86,88
The Crofts..17,53, 103
Corn Street 17,18,22,32,55,74, 79,81,83,101,102, 103,114,117,118, 119,123,124,125, 126
Corndell.....18,22
Crown Lane....20
Curbridge Road 41,72,79
Davenport Road 74
Deer Park Road 22
Downs Road....80
Duck Alley..17,26
Gloucester Place 119
Harcourt Street 59
High Street 38,40,51,71,75,80, 101,103,105,114, 115,119
Highworth Place 109
The Hill....42,112
Holloway Road 81,126
Langdale Gate 20,89
Market Place 79,83,101
Market Square 79,83,87,97,117, 118,119,124,125
Marlborough Lane 69,74,127
Meeting House Lane......... 69,74
Mill Street 59,96,115
Narrow Hill....39
Oxford Hill 86,132
Queen Emma's Dyke.............19
Tower Hill.33,114
Welch Way 105,131
West End 11,22,40,61,81,86

93,96,101,102, 112,114,115,118, 131
Wood Green 39,55,65,67,68, 69,71,78,86,95, 102,112,118
Woodstock Road 67,80
Street, George E...64
Strickland, Walter 87
Swinford Toll Bridge 85
swimming pools 77,82,130
Tarrant & Sons 117,118,125
William....... 117
Taunton...........101
Technical College 42
Temperance Hotel 75,79
Societies........79
Temple Guiting....20
tenters..........48,58
Thames...49,85,86 Valley............13
Thames and Severn Canal...............86
theatre..........79,80
Threfts.............30
Tiger Moths........96
Timson, Mr........85
Tite's, Messrs......80
toll house, West End 86
Tomson, George..29
tournaments.......77
Townsend, William 34,35
Trade Commissioners 48,49
Trade Fair..120,132
Tyrie, James.......30
Unterhaching....131
Up-towns..........78
Urban District Council......103,104
Valentine & Barrell 118
Vestry.............102
Victory in Europe Day.................98
Waitrose...118,131
Walker's (Yorkshire blanket company).53
Waller, General...93

War Memorial.....95
Ward Beyond the Bridge.............101
Warfordsleigh.....22
Warring family.....93
Warrington, Mr..117
water tower..103,104
Wellington, Duke of 51
Wenman
Chapel 40
family...........91
Richard........111
Wesley, John 70,71,85
Wesleyans......64,79
Westminster.......22
West Oxfordshire College..........18,42
West Oxfordshire District Council..131
West Ward........101
Whitlock, Elisha...49
Wilkinson,
George 33,114
William 28,33,34, 73,105,114,115
Williams, George 118
Wilmot, Edward 111,112
Winchester,
Bishops of 29,47, 63,77,78,91, 111,115
Alfwine..........18
Blois, Henry of 20,91
Gardiner........23
Ponet, John.....23
Roches, Peter des 20,21,63,101
Stigand..........20
Trelawney, Sir Jonathan........62
Winchester Cathedral..........19
Windrush
River 13,14,15,17, 18,20,21,47,48,49, 65,78,82,85,86, 100,108,131
Valley..........103
Windrush Valley Estate...........22
Housing Association 119
Witan................13
Witenie............ 13
Witney Blanket Company.....53,118

Witney Blanket Industry, The..,....48
Witney Gazette 31,77,80,94, 103,105,119
Witney
Chess Club......78
Debating Society 130
Dramatic Society 80,131
Railway Company 87
Witney Trips 76,77,78
Witta............13,17
Wittanige/Wyttanige/ Wyttenige...13,17,18
Women's
Institute 95
Voluntary Service 95
Wood, Dr William Dyson.............103
Woodstock.....21,93
Woolgate.........118
woollen industry 47-53
workhouse.....31,32, 33,114
World War I...78,93, 98,104,109
World War II...80,87, 94,95,96,98,100, 114117,119,131
Worsham waterworks......104
Wright, John.......40
Wychwood Forest 13,22,77
Yates
family..........112
Robert..........66
Yarnton............87
Young, Arthur 48,51,85

138